Programming Embedded Systems
in C and C++

Programming Embedded Systems
in C and C++

Michael Barr

O'REILLY®

Beijing · Cambridge · Köln · Paris · Sebastopol · Taipei · Tokyo

Programming Embedded Systems in C and C++
by Michael Barr

Copyright © 1999 O'Reilly & Associates, Inc. All rights reserved.
Printed in the United States of America.

Published by O'Reilly & Associates, Inc., 101 Morris Street, Sebastopol, CA 95472.

Editor: Andy Oram

Production Editor: Melanie Wang

Printing History:

        January 1999:   First Edition.

This book is printed on acid-free paper with 85% recycled content, 15% post-consumer waste. O'Reilly & Associates is committed to using paper with the highest recycled content available consistent with high quality.

ISBN: 1-56592-354-5

For Mom and Dad

Table of Contents

Preface .... *xi*

1. **Introduction** *1*
   What Is an Embedded System? *1*
   Variations on the Theme *4*
   C: The Least Common Denominator *9*
   A Few Words About Hardware *11*

2. **Your First Embedded Program** *13*
   Hello, World! *13*
   Das Blinkenlights *14*
   The Role of the Infinite Loop *18*

3. **Compiling, Linking, and Locating** *19*
   The Build Process *19*
   Compiling *21*
   Linking *23*
   Locating *25*
   Building das Blinkenlights *27*

4. **Downloading and Debugging** *30*
   When in ROM... .... *30*
   Remote Debuggers *32*
   Emulators *35*
   Simulators and Other Tools *37*

5. *Getting to Know the Hardware* *40*
Understand the Big Picture *40*
Examine the Landscape *42*
Learn How to Communicate *47*
Get to Know the Processor *50*
Study the External Peripherals *53*
Initialize the Hardware *54*

6. *Memory* *57*
Types of Memory *57*
Memory Testing *61*
Validating Memory Contents *74*
Working with Flash Memory *79*

7. *Peripherals* *84*
Control and Status Registers *84*
The Device Driver Philosophy *86*
A Simple Timer Driver *89*
Das Blinkenlights, Revisited *97*

8. *Operating Systems* *100*
History and Purpose *100*
A Decent Embedded Operating System *101*
Real-Time Characteristics *119*
Selection Process *122*

9. *Putting It All Together* *124*
Application Overview *124*
Flashing the LED *126*
Printing "Hello, World!" *130*
Working with Serial Ports *131*
The Zilog 85230 Serial Controller *137*

10. *Optimizing Your Code* *139*
Increasing Code Efficiency *139*
Decreasing Code Size *143*
Reducing Memory Usage *144*
Limiting the Impact of C++ *146*

Appendix: Arcom's Target188EB *149*

Glossary *151*

Bibliography *165*

Index *169*

Preface

*First figure out why you want the students to learn
the subject and what you want them to know,
and the method will result more or less
by common sense.*

—Richard Feynman

Embedded software is in almost every electronic device in use today. There is software hidden away inside our watches, VCRs, cellular phones, and even a few toasters. The military uses embedded software to guide missiles and detect enemy aircraft. And communication satellites, deep-space probes, and many medical instruments would've been nearly impossible to create without it.

Someone has to write all that software, and there are tens of thousands of electrical engineers, computer scientists, and other professionals who actually do. I am one of them, and I know from my personal experience just how hard it can be to learn the craft. There aren't any embedded software courses in school, and I've never been able to find a decent book about the subject in any library.

Each embedded system is unique, and the hardware is highly specialized to the application domain. As a result, embedded systems programming can be a widely varying experience and can take years to master. However, one common denominator across almost all embedded software development is the use of the C programming language. This book will teach you how to use C and its descendent C++ in any embedded system.

Even if you already know how to write embedded software, you can still learn a lot from this book. In addition to learning how to use C and C++ more effectively, you'll also benefit from the detailed explanations and source code solutions to common embedded software problems. Among the advanced topics covered in the book are memory testing and verification, device driver design and implementation, real-time operating system internals, and code optimization techniques.

Why I Wrote This Book

I once heard an estimate that in the United States there are eight microprocessor-based devices for every person. At the time, I wondered how this could be. Are there really that many computers surrounding us? Later, when I had more time to think about it, I started to make a list of the things I used that probably contained a microprocessor. Within five minutes, my list contained ten items: television, stereo, coffee maker, alarm clock, VCR, microwave, dishwasher, remote control, bread machine, and digital watch. And those were just my personal possessions—I quickly came up with ten more devices I used at work.

The revelation that every one of those products contains not only a processor, but also software, was not far behind. At last, I knew what I wanted to do with my life. I wanted to put my programming skills to work developing embedded computer systems. But how would I acquire the necessary knowledge? At this point, I was in my last year of college. There hadn't been any classes on embedded systems programming so far, and I wasn't able to find any listed in the course catalog.

Fortunately, when I graduated I found a company that let me write embedded software while I was still learning. But I was pretty much on my own. The few people who knew about embedded software were usually too busy to explain things to me, so I searched high and low for a book that would teach me. In the end, I found I had to learn everything myself. I never found that book, and I always wondered why no one had written it.

Now I've decided to write that book myself. And in the process, I've discovered why no one had done it before. One of the hardest things about this subject is knowing when to stop writing. Each embedded system is unique, and I have learned that there is an exception to every rule. Nevertheless, I have tried to boil the subject down to its essence and present only those things that programmers definitely need to know about embedded systems.

Intended Audience

This is a book about programming embedded systems in C and C++. As such, it assumes that the reader already has some programming experience and is at least familiar with the syntax of these two languages. It also helps if you have some familiarity with basic data structures, such as linked lists. The book does not assume that you have a great deal of knowledge about computer hardware, but it does expect that you are willing to learn a little bit about hardware along the way. This is, after all, a part of the job of an embedded programmer.

While writing this book, I had two types of readers in mind. The first reader is a beginner—much as I was when I graduated from college. She has a background in computer science or engineering and a few years of programming experience. The beginner is interested in writing embedded software for a living but is not sure just how to get started. After reading the first five chapters, she will be able to put her programming skills to work developing simple embedded programs. The rest of the book will act as her reference for the more advanced topics encountered in the coming months and years of her career.

The second reader is already an embedded systems programmer. She is familiar with embedded hardware and knows how to write software for it but is looking for a reference book that explains key topics. Perhaps the embedded systems programmer has experience only with assembly language programming and is relatively new to C and C++. In that case, the book will teach her how to use those languages in an embedded system, and the later chapters will provide the advanced material she requires.

Whether you fall into one of these categories or not, I hope this book provides the information you are looking for in a format that is friendly and easily accessible.

Organization

The book contains ten chapters, one appendix, a glossary, and an annotated bibliography. The ten chapters can be divided quite nicely into two parts. The first part consists of Chapters 1 through 5 and is intended mainly for newcomers to embedded systems. These chapters should be read in their entirety and in the order that they appear. This will bring you up to speed quickly and introduce you to the basics of embedded software development. After completing Chapter 5, you will be ready to develop small pieces of embedded software on your own.

The second part of the book consists of Chapters 6 through 10 and discusses advanced topics that are of interest to inexperienced and experienced embedded programmers alike. These chapters are mostly self-contained and can be read in any order. In addition, Chapters 6 through 9 contain example programs that might be useful to you on a future embedded software project.

- Chapter 1, *Introduction*, introduces you to embedded systems. It defines the term, gives examples, and explains why C and C++ were selected as the languages of the book.

- Chapter 2, *Your First Embedded Program*, walks you through the process of writing a simple embedded program in C. This is roughly the equivalent of the "Hello, World" example presented in most other programming books.

- Chapter 3, *Compiling, Linking, and Locating*, introduces the software development tools you will be using to prepare your programs for execution by an embedded processor.

- Chapter 4, *Downloading and Debugging*, presents various techniques for loading your executable programs into an embedded system. It also describes the debugging tools and techniques that are available to you.

- Chapter 5, *Getting to Know the Hardware*, outlines a simple procedure for learning about unfamiliar hardware platforms. After completing this chapter, you will be ready to write and debug simple embedded programs.

- Chapter 6, *Memory*, tells you everything you need to know about memory in embedded systems. The chapter includes source code implementations of memory tests and Flash memory drivers.

- Chapter 7, *Peripherals*, explains device driver design and implementation techniques and includes an example driver for a common peripheral called a timer.

- Chapter 8, *Operating Systems*, includes a very basic operating system that can be used in any embedded system. It also helps you decide if you'll need an operating system at all and, if so, whether to buy one or write your own.

- Chapter 9, *Putting It All Together*, expands on the device driver and operating system concepts presented in the previous chapters. It explains how to control more complicated peripherals and includes a complete example application that pulls together everything you've learned so far.

- Chapter 10, *Optimizing Your Code*, explains how to simultaneously increase the speed and decrease the memory requirements of your embedded software. This includes tips for taking advantage of the most beneficial C++ features without paying a significant performance penalty.

Throughout the book, I have tried to strike a balance between specific examples and general knowledge. Whenever possible, I have eliminated minor details in the hopes of making the book more readable. You will gain the most from the book if you view the examples, as I do, only as tools for understanding important concepts. Try not to get bogged down in the details of any one circuit board or chip. If you understand the general concepts, you should be able to apply them to any embedded system you encounter.

Conventions, Typographical and Otherwise

The following typographical conventions are used throughout the book:

Italic

is used for the names of files, functions, programs, methods, routines, and options when they appear in the body of a paragraph. Italic is also used for emphasis and to introduce new terms.

`Constant Width`

is used in the examples to show the contents of files and the output of commands. In the body of a paragraph, this style is used for keywords, variable names, classes, objects, parameters, and other code snippets.

`Constant Width Bold`

is used in the examples to show commands and options that you type literally.

The owl symbol is used to indicate a tip, suggestion, or general note.

The turkey symbol is used to indicate a warning.

Other conventions relate to gender and roles. With respect to gender, I have purposefully alternated my use of the terms "he" and "she" throughout the book. "He" is used in the odd-numbered chapters and "she" in all of the even-numbered ones.

With respect to roles, I have occasionally distinguished between the tasks of hardware engineers, embedded software engineers, and application programmers in my discussion. But these titles refer only to roles played by individual engineers, and it should be noted that it can and often does happen that one individual fills more than one of these roles.

Obtaining the Examples Online

This book includes many source code listing, and all but the most trivial one-liners are available online. These examples are organized by chapter number and include build instructions (makefiles) to help you recreate each of the executables. The complete archive is available via FTP, at *ftp://ftp.oreilly.com/examples/ nutshell/embedded_c/*.

How to Contact Us

We have tested and verified all the information in this book to the best of our ability, but you may find that features have changed (or even that we have made mistakes!). Please let us know about any errors you find, as well as your suggestions for future editions, by writing to:

O'Reilly & Associates
101 Morris Street
Sebastopol, CA 95472
800-998-9938 (in the U.S. or Canada)
707-829-0515 (international/local)
707-829-0104 (FAX)

You can also send messages electronically. To be put on our mailing list or to request a catalog, send email to:

nuts@oreilly.com

To ask technical questions or to comment on the book, send email to:

bookquestions@oreilly.com

Personal Comments and Acknowledgments

As long as I can remember I have been interested in writing a book or two. But now that I have done so, I must confess that I was naive when I started. I had no idea how much work it would take, nor how many other people would have to get involved. Another thing that surprised me was how easy it was to find a willing publisher. I had expected that to be the hard part.

From proposal to publication, this project has taken almost two years to complete. But, then, that's mostly because I worked a full-time job throughout and tried to maintain as much of my social life as possible. Had I known when I started that I'd still be agonizing over final drafts at this late date, I would have probably quit working and finished the book more quickly. But continuing to work has been good for the book (as well as my bank account!). It has allowed me the luxury of discussing my ideas regularly with a complete cast of embedded hardware and software professionals. Many of these same folks have also contributed to the book more directly by reviewing drafts of some or all of the chapters.

I am indebted to all of the following people for sharing their ideas and reviewing my work: Toby Bennett, Paul Cabler (and the other great folks at Arcom), Mike Corish, Kevin D'Souza, Don Davis, Steve Edwards, Mike Ficco, Barbara Flanagan, Jack Ganssle, Stephen Harpster (who christened me "King of the Sentence Fragment" after reading an early draft), Jonathan Harris, Jim Jensen, Mark Kohler, Andy Kollegger, Jeff Mallory, Ian Miller, Henry Neugauss, Chris Schanck, Brian Silverman, John Snyder, Jason Steinhorn (whose constant stream of grammatical and technical critiques have made this book worth reading), Ian Taylor, Lindsey Vereen, Jeff Whipple, and Greg Young.

I would also like to thank my editor, Andy Oram. Without his enthusiasm for my initial proposal, overabundant patience, and constant encouragement, this book would never have been completed.

Finally, I'd like to thank Alpa Dharia for her support and encouragement throughout this long process.

Michael Barr
mbarr@netrino.com

In this chapter:
- **What Is an Embedded System?**
- **Variations on the Theme**
- **C: The Least Common Denominator**
- **A Few Words About Hardware**

1

Introduction

I think there is a world market for maybe five computers.
—Thomas Watson, Chairman of IBM, 1943

There is no reason anyone would want a computer in their home.
—Ken Olson, President of Digital Equipment Corporation, 1977

One of the more surprising developments of the last few decades has been the ascendance of computers to a position of prevalence in human affairs. Today there are more computers in our homes and offices than there are people who live and work in them. Yet many of these computers are not recognized as such by their users. In this chapter, I'll explain what embedded systems are and where they are found. I will also introduce the subject of embedded programming, explain why I have selected C and C++ as the languages for this book, and describe the hardware used in the examples.

What Is an Embedded System?

An *embedded system* is a combination of computer hardware and software, and perhaps additional mechanical or other parts, designed to perform a specific function. A good example is the microwave oven. Almost every household has one, and tens of millions of them are used every day, but very few people realize that a processor and software are involved in the preparation of their lunch or dinner.

This is in direct contrast to the personal computer in the family room. It too is comprised of computer hardware and software and mechanical components (disk drives, for example). However, a personal computer is not designed to perform a specific function. Rather, it is able to do many different things. Many people use the term *general-purpose computer* to make this distinction clear. As shipped, a

1

general-purpose computer is a blank slate; the manufacturer does not know what the customer will do with it. One customer may use it for a network file server, another may use it exclusively for playing games, and a third may use it to write the next great American novel.

Frequently, an embedded system is a component within some larger system. For example, modern cars and trucks contain many embedded systems. One embedded system controls the anti-lock brakes, another monitors and controls the vehicle's emissions, and a third displays information on the dashboard. In some cases, these embedded systems are connected by some sort of a communications network, but that is certainly not a requirement.

At the possible risk of confusing you, it is important to point out that a general-purpose computer is itself made up of numerous embedded systems. For example, my computer consists of a keyboard, mouse, video card, modem, hard drive, floppy drive, and sound card—each of which is an embedded system. Each of these devices contains a processor and software and is designed to perform a specific function. For example, the modem is designed to send and receive digital data over an analog telephone line. That's it. And all of the other devices can be summarized in a single sentence as well.

If an embedded system is designed well, the existence of the processor and software could be completely unnoticed by a user of the device. Such is the case for a microwave oven, VCR, or alarm clock. In some cases, it would even be possible to build an equivalent device that does not contain the processor and software. This could be done by replacing the combination with a custom integrated circuit that performs the same functions in hardware. However, a lot of flexibility is lost when a design is hard-coded in this way. It is much easier, and cheaper, to change a few lines of software than to redesign a piece of custom hardware.

History and Future

Given the definition of embedded systems earlier in this chapter, the first such systems could not possibly have appeared before 1971. That was the year Intel introduced the world's first microprocessor. This chip, the 4004, was designed for use in a line of business calculators produced by the Japanese company Busicom. In 1969, Busicom asked Intel to design a set of custom integrated circuits—one for each of their new calculator models. The 4004 was Intel's response. Rather than design custom hardware for each calculator, Intel proposed a general-purpose circuit that could be used throughout the entire line of calculators. This general-purpose processor was designed to read and execute a set of instructions—software—stored in an external memory chip. Intel's idea was that the software would give each calculator its unique set of features.

The microprocessor was an overnight success, and its use increased steadily over the next decade. Early embedded applications included unmanned space probes, computerized traffic lights, and aircraft flight control systems. In the 1980s, embedded systems quietly rode the waves of the microcomputer age and brought microprocessors into every part of our personal and professional lives. Many of the electronic devices in our kitchens (bread machines, food processors, and microwave ovens), living rooms (televisions, stereos, and remote controls), and workplaces (fax machines, pagers, laser printers, cash registers, and credit card readers) are embedded systems.

It seems inevitable that the number of embedded systems will continue to increase rapidly. Already there are promising new embedded devices that have enormous market potential: light switches and thermostats that can be controlled by a central computer, intelligent air-bag systems that don't inflate when children or small adults are present, palm-sized electronic organizers and personal digital assistants (PDAs), digital cameras, and dashboard navigation systems. Clearly, individuals who possess the skills and desire to design the next generation of embedded systems will be in demand for quite some time.

Real-Time Systems

One subclass of embedded systems is worthy of an introduction at this point. As commonly defined, a *real-time system* is a computer system that has timing constraints. In other words, a real-time system is partly specified in terms of its ability to make certain calculations or decisions in a timely manner. These important calculations are said to have deadlines for completion. And, for all practical purposes, a missed deadline is just as bad as a wrong answer.

The issue of what happens if a deadline is missed is a crucial one. For example, if the real-time system is part of an airplane's flight control system, it is possible for the lives of the passengers and crew to be endangered by a single missed deadline. However, if instead the system is involved in satellite communication, the damage could be limited to a single corrupt data packet. The more severe the consequences, the more likely it will be said that the deadline is "hard" and, thus, the system a hard real-time system. Real-time systems at the other end of this continuum are said to have "soft" deadlines.

All of the topics and examples presented in this book are applicable to the designers of real-time systems. However, the designer of a real-time system must be more diligent in his work. He must guarantee reliable operation of the software and hardware under all possible conditions. And, to the degree that human lives depend upon the system's proper execution, this guarantee must be backed by engineering calculations and descriptive paperwork.

Variations on the Theme

Unlike software designed for general-purpose computers, embedded software cannot usually be run on other embedded systems without significant modification. This is mainly because of the incredible variety in the underlying hardware. The hardware in each embedded system is tailored specifically to the application, in order to keep system costs low. As a result, unnecessary circuitry is eliminated and hardware resources are shared wherever possible. In this section you will learn what hardware features are common across all embedded systems and why there is so much variation with respect to just about everything else.

By definition all embedded systems contain a processor and software, but what other features do they have in common? Certainly, in order to have software, there must be a place to store the executable code and temporary storage for runtime data manipulation. These take the form of ROM and RAM, respectively; any embedded system will have some of each. If only a small amount of memory is required, it might be contained within the same chip as the processor. Otherwise, one or both types of memory will reside in external memory chips.

All embedded systems also contain some type of inputs and outputs. For example, in a microwave oven the inputs are the buttons on the front panel and a temperature probe, and the outputs are the human-readable display and the microwave radiation. It is almost always the case that the outputs of the embedded system are a function of its inputs and several other factors (elapsed time, current temperature, etc.). The inputs to the system usually take the form of sensors and probes, communication signals, or control knobs and buttons. The outputs are typically displays, communication signals, or changes to the physical world. See Figure 1-1 for a general example of an embedded system.

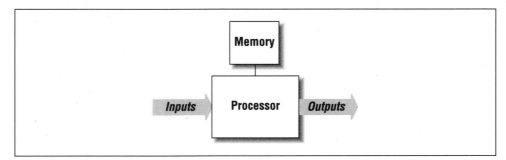

Figure 1-1. A generic embedded system

With the exception of these few common features, the rest of the embedded hardware is usually unique. This variation is the result of many competing design criteria. Each system must meet a completely different set of requirements, any or all of which can affect the compromises and tradeoffs made during the development of the product. For example, if the system must have a production cost of less than $10, then other things—like processing power and system reliability—might need to be sacrificed in order to meet that goal.

Of course, production cost is only one of the possible constraints under which embedded hardware designers work. Other common design requirements include the following:

Processing power

The amount of processing power necessary to get the job done. A common way to compare processing power is the MIPS (millions of instructions per second) rating. If two processors have ratings of 25 MIPS and 40 MIPS, the latter is said to be the more powerful of the two. However, other important features of the processor need to be considered. One of these is the register width, which typically ranges from 8 to 64 bits. Today's general-purpose computers use 32- and 64-bit processors exclusively, but embedded systems are still commonly built with older and less costly 8- and 16-bit processors.

Memory

The amount of memory (ROM and RAM) required to hold the executable software and the data it manipulates. Here the hardware designer must usually make his best estimate up front and be prepared to increase or decrease the actual amount as the software is being developed. The amount of memory required can also affect the processor selection. In general, the register width of a processor establishes the upper limit of the amount of memory it can access (e.g., an 8-bit address register can select one of only 256 unique memory locations).*

Development cost

The cost of the hardware and software design processes. This is a fixed, one-time cost, so it might be that money is no object (usually for high-volume products) or that this is the only accurate measure of system cost (in the case of a small number of units produced).

Number of units

The tradeoff between production cost and development cost is affected most by the number of units expected to be produced and sold. For example, it is usually undesirable to develop your own custom hardware components for a low-volume product.

---

* Of course, the smaller the register width, the more likely it is that the processor employs tricks like multiple address spaces to support more memory. A few hundred bytes just isn't enough to do much of anything. Several thousand bytes is a more likely minimum, even for an 8-bit processor.

Expected lifetime

> How long must the system continue to function (on average)? A month, a year, or a decade? This affects all sorts of design decisions from the selection of hardware components to how much the system may cost to develop and produce.

Reliability

> How reliable must the final product be? If it is a children's toy, it doesn't always have to work right, but if it's a part of a space shuttle or a car, it had sure better do what it is supposed to each and every time.

In addition to these general requirements, there are the detailed functional requirements of the system itself. These are the things that give the embedded system its unique identity as a microwave oven, pacemaker, or pager.

Table 1-1 illustrates the range of possible values for each of the previous design requirements. These are only estimates and should not be taken too seriously. In some cases, two or more of the criteria are linked. For example, increases in processing power could lead to increased production costs. Conversely, we might imagine that the same increase in processing power would have the effect of decreasing the development costs—by reducing the complexity of the hardware and software design. So the values in a particular column do not necessarily go together.

Table 1-1. Common Design Requirements for Embedded Systems

Criterion	Low	Medium	High
Processor	4- or 8-bit	16-bit	32- or 64-bit
Memory	< 16 KB	64 KB to 1 MB	> 1 MB
Development cost	< $100,000	$100,000 to $1,000,000	> $1,000,000
Production cost	< $10	$10 to $1,000	> $1,000
Number of units	< 100	100–10,000	> 10,000
Expected lifetime	days, weeks, or months	years	decades
Reliability	may occasionally fail	must work reliably	must be fail-proof

In order to simultaneously demonstrate the variation from one embedded system to the next and the possible effects of these design requirements on the hardware, I will now take some time to describe three embedded systems in some detail. My goal is to put you in the system designer's shoes for a few moments before beginning to narrow our discussion to embedded software development.

Digital Watch

At the end of the evolutionary path that began with sundials, water clocks, and hourglasses is the digital watch. Among its many features are the presentation of the date and time (usually to the nearest second), the measurement of the length of an event to the nearest hundredth of a second, and the generation of an annoying little sound at the beginning of each hour. As it turns out, these are very simple tasks that do not require very much processing power or memory. In fact, the only reason to employ a processor at all is to support a range of models and features from a single hardware design.

The typical digital watch contains a simple, inexpensive 8-bit processor. Because such small processors cannot address very much memory, this type of processor usually contains its own on-chip ROM. And, if there are sufficient registers available, this application may not require any RAM at all. In fact, all of the electronics—processor, memory, counters and real-time clocks—are likely to be stored in a single chip. The only other hardware elements of the watch are the inputs (buttons) and outputs (LCD and speaker).

The watch designer's goal is to create a reasonably reliable product that has an extraordinarily low production cost. If, after production, some watches are found to keep more reliable time than most, they can be sold under a brand name with a higher markup. Otherwise, a profit can still be made by selling the watch through a discount sales channel. For lower-cost versions, the stopwatch buttons or speaker could be eliminated. This would limit the functionality of the watch but might not even require any software changes. And, of course, the cost of all this development effort may be fairly high, since it will be amortized over hundreds of thousands or even millions of watch sales.

Video Game Player

When you pull the Nintendo-64 or Sony Playstation out from your entertainment center, you are preparing to use an embedded system. In some cases, these machines are more powerful than the comparable generation of personal computers. Yet video game players for the home market are relatively inexpensive compared to personal computers. It is the competing requirements of high processing power and low production cost that keep video game designers awake at night (and their children well-fed).

The companies that produce video game players don't usually care how much it costs to develop the system, so long as the production costs of the resulting product are low—typically around a hundred dollars. They might even encourage their engineers to design custom processors at a development cost of hundreds of thousands of dollars each. So, although there might be a 64-bit processor inside your video game player, it is not necessarily the same type of processor that would be found in a 64-bit personal computer. In all likelihood, the processor is highly specialized for the demands of the video games it is intended to play.

Because production cost is so crucial in the home video game market, the designers also use tricks to shift the costs around. For example, one common tactic is to move as much of the memory and other peripheral electronics as possible off of the main circuit board and onto the game cartridges. This helps to reduce the cost of the game player, but increases the price of each and every game. So, while the system might have a powerful 64-bit processor, it might have only a few megabytes of memory on the main circuit board. This is just enough memory to bootstrap the machine to a state from which it can access additional memory on the game cartridge.

Mars Explorer

In 1976, two unmanned spacecraft arrived on the planet Mars. As part of their mission, they were to collect samples of the Martian surface, analyze the chemical makeup of each, and transmit the results to scientists back on Earth. Those Viking missions are amazing to me. Surrounded by personal computers that must be rebooted almost daily, I find it remarkable that more than 20 years ago a team of scientists and engineers successfully built two computers that survived a journey of 34 million miles and functioned correctly for half a decade. Clearly, reliability was one of the most important requirements for these systems.

What if a memory chip had failed? Or the software had bugs that caused it to crash? Or an electrical connection broke during impact? There is no way to prevent such problems from occurring. So, all of these potential failure points and many others had to be eliminated by adding redundant circuitry or extra functionality: an extra processor here, special memory diagnostics there, a hardware timer to reset the system if the software got stuck, and so on.

More recently, NASA launched the Pathfinder mission. Its primary goal was to demonstrate the feasibility of getting to Mars on a budget. Of course, given the advances in technology made since the mid-70s, the designers didn't have to give up too much to accomplish this. They might have reduced the amount of redundancy somewhat, but they still gave Pathfinder more processing power and memory than Viking ever could have. The Mars Pathfinder was actually two embedded systems: a landing craft and a rover. The landing craft had a 32-bit processor and 128 MB of RAM; the rover, on the other hand, had only an 8-bit processor and 512 KB. These choices probably reflect the different functional requirements of the two systems. But I'm sure that production cost wasn't much of an issue in either case.

C: The Least Common Denominator

One of the few constants across all these systems is the use of the C programming language. More than any other, C has become the language of embedded programmers. This has not always been the case, and it will not continue to be so forever. However, at this time, C is the closest thing there is to a standard in the embedded world. In this section I'll explain why C has become so popular and why I have chosen it and its descendent C++ as the primary languages of this book.

Because successful software development is so frequently about selecting the best language for a given project, it is surprising to find that one language has proven itself appropriate for both 8-bit and 64-bit processors; in systems with bytes, kilobytes, and megabytes of memory; and for development teams that consist of from one to a dozen or more people. Yet this is precisely the range of projects in which C has thrived.

Of course, C is not without advantages. It is small and fairly simple to learn, compilers are available for almost every processor in use today, and there is a very large body of experienced C programmers. In addition, C has the benefit of processor-independence, which allows programmers to concentrate on algorithms and applications, rather than on the details of a particular processor architecture. However, many of these advantages apply equally to other high-level languages. So why has C succeeded where so many other languages have largely failed?

Perhaps the greatest strength of C—and the thing that sets it apart from languages like Pascal and FORTRAN—is that it is a very "low-level" high-level language. As we shall see throughout the book, C gives embedded programmers an extraordinary degree of direct hardware control without sacrificing the benefits of high-level languages. The "low-level" nature of C was a clear intention of the language's creators. In fact, Kernighan and Ritchie included the following comment in the opening pages of their book *The C Programming Language*:

> C is a relatively "low level" language. This characterization is not pejorative; it simply means that C deals with the same sort of objects that most computers do. These may be combined and moved about with the arithmetic and logical operators implemented by real machines.

Few popular high-level languages can compete with C in the production of compact, efficient code for almost all processors. And, of these, only C allows programmers to interact with the underlying hardware so easily.

Other Embedded Languages

Of course, C is not the only language used by embedded programmers. At least three other languages—assembly, C++, and Ada—are worth mentioning in greater detail.

In the early days, embedded software was written exclusively in the assembly language of the target processor. This gave programmers complete control of the processor and other hardware, but at a price. Assembly languages have many disadvantages, not the least of which are higher software development costs and a lack of code portability. In addition, finding skilled assembly programmers has become much more difficult in recent years. Assembly is now used primarily as an adjunct to the high-level language, usually only for those small pieces of code that must be extremely efficient or ultra-compact, or cannot be written in any other way.

C++ is an object-oriented superset of C that is increasingly popular among embedded programmers. All of the core language features are the same as C, but C++ adds new functionality for better data abstraction and a more object-oriented style of programming. These new features are very helpful to software developers, but some of them do reduce the efficiency of the executable program. So C++ tends to be most popular with large development teams, where the benefits to developers outweigh the loss of program efficiency.

Ada is also an object-oriented language, though it is substantially different than C++. Ada was originally designed by the U.S. Department of Defense for the development of mission-critical military software. Despite being twice accepted as an international standard (Ada83 and Ada95), it has not gained much of a foothold outside of the defense and aerospace industries. And it is losing ground there in recent years. This is unfortunate because the Ada language has many features that would simplify embedded software development if used instead of C++.

Choosing a Language for the Book

A major question facing the author of a book like this is, which programming languages should be included in the discussion? Attempting to cover too many languages might confuse the reader or detract from more important points. On the other hand, focusing too narrowly could make the discussion unnecessarily academic or (worse for the author and publisher) limit the potential market for the book.

Certainly, C must be the centerpiece of any book about embedded programming—and this book will be no exception. More than half of the sample code is written in C, and the discussion will focus primarily on C-related programming issues. Of course, everything that is said about C programming applies equally to

C++. In addition, I will cover those features of C++ that are most useful for embedded software development and use them in the later examples. Assembly language will be discussed in certain limited contexts, but will be avoided whenever possible. In other words, I will mention assembly language only when a particular programming task cannot be accomplished in any other way.

I feel that this mixed treatment of C, C++, and assembly most accurately reflects how embedded software is actually developed today and how it will continue to be developed in the near-term future. I hope that this choice will keep the discussion clear, provide information that is useful to people developing actual systems, and include as large a potential audience as possible.

A Few Words About Hardware

It is the nature of programming that books about the subject must include examples. Typically, these examples are selected so that they can be easily experimented with by interested readers. That means readers must have access to the very same software development tools and hardware platforms used by the author. Unfortunately, in the case of embedded programming, this is unrealistic. It simply does not make sense to run any of the example programs on the platforms available to most readers—PCs, Macs, and Unix workstations.

Even selecting a standard embedded platform is difficult. As you have already learned, there is no such thing as a "typical" embedded system. Whatever hardware is selected, the majority of readers will not have access to it. But despite this rather significant problem, I do feel it is important to select a reference hardware platform for use in the examples. In so doing, I hope to make the examples consistent and, thus, the entire discussion more clear.

In order to illustrate as many points as possible with a single piece of hardware, I have found it necessary to select a middle-of-the-road platform. This hardware consists of a 16-bit processor (Intel's 80188EB*), a decent amount of memory (128 KB of RAM and 256 KB of ROM), and some common types of inputs, outputs, and peripheral components. The board I've chosen is called the Target188EB and is manufactured and sold by Arcom Control Systems. More information about the Arcom board and instructions for obtaining one can be found in the appendix, *Arcom's Target188EB*.

---

* Intel's 80188EB processor is a special version of the 80186 that has been redesigned for use in embedded systems. The original 80186 was a successor to the 8086 processor that IBM used in their very first personal computer—the PC/XT. The 80186 was never the basis of any PC because it was passed over (in favor of the 80286) when IBM designed their next model—the PC/AT. Despite that early failure, versions of the 80186 from Intel and AMD have enjoyed tremendous success in embedded systems in recent years.

If you have access to the reference hardware, you will be able to work through the examples in the book exactly as they are presented. Otherwise, you will need to port the example code to an embedded platform that you do have access to. Toward that end, every effort has been made to make the example programs as portable as possible. However, the reader should bear in mind that the hardware in each embedded system is different and that some of the examples might be meaningless on his hardware. For example, it wouldn't make sense to port the Flash memory driver presented in Chapter 6, *Memory*, to a board that had no Flash memory devices.

Anyway I'll have a lot more to say about hardware in Chapter 5, *Getting to Know the Hardware*. But first we have a number of software issues to discuss. So let's get started.

In this chapter:
- *Hello, World!*
- *Das Blinkenlights*
- *The Role of the Infinite Loop*

2

Your First Embedded Program

ACHTUNG! Das machine is nicht fur gefingerpoken und mittengrabben. Ist easy schnappen der springenwerk, blowenfusen und corkenpoppen mit spitzensparken. Ist nicht fur gewerken by das dummkopfen. Das rubbernecken sightseeren keepen hands in das pockets. Relaxen und vatch das blinkenlights!

In this chapter we'll dive right into embedded programming by way of an example. The program we'll look at is similar in spirit to the "Hello, World!" example found in the beginning of most other programming books. As we discuss the code, I'll provide justification for the selection of the particular program and point out the parts of it that are dependent on the target hardware. This chapter contains only the source code for this first program. We'll discuss how to create the executable and actually run it in the two chapters that follow.

Hello, World!

It seems like every programming book ever written begins with the same example—a program that prints "Hello, World!" on the user's screen. An overused example like this might seem a bit boring. But it does help readers to quickly assess the ease or difficulty with which simple programs can be written in the programming environment at hand. In that sense, "Hello, World!" serves as a useful benchmark of programming languages and computer platforms. Unfortunately, by this measure, embedded systems are among the most difficult computer platforms for programmers to work with. In some embedded systems, it might even be impossible to implement the "Hello, World!" program. And in those systems that are capable of supporting it, the printing of text strings is usually more of an endpoint than a beginning.

You see, the underlying assumption of the "Hello, World!" example is that there is some sort of output device on which strings of characters can be printed. A text window on the user's monitor often serves that purpose. But most embedded systems lack a monitor or analogous output device. And those that do have one typically require a special piece of embedded software, called a display driver, to be implemented first—a rather challenging way to begin one's embedded programming career.

It would be much better to begin with a small, easily implemented, and highly portable embedded program in which there is little room for programming mistakes. After all, the reason my book-writing counterparts continue to use the "Hello, World!" example is that it is a no-brainer to implement. This eliminates one of the variables if the reader's program doesn't work right the first time: it isn't a bug in their code; rather, it is a problem with the development tools or process that they used to create the executable program.

Embedded programmers must be self-reliant. They must always begin each new project with the assumption that nothing works—that all they can rely on is the basic syntax of their programming language. Even the standard library routines might not be available to them. These are the auxiliary functions—like *printf* and *scanf*—that most other programmers take for granted. In fact, library routines are often as much a part of the language standard as the basic syntax. However, that part of the standard is more difficult to support across all possible computing platforms and is occasionally ignored by the makers of compilers for embedded systems.

So you won't find an actual "Hello, World!" program in this chapter. Instead, we will assume only the basic syntax of C is available for our first example. As we progress through the book, we will gradually add C++ syntax, standard library routines, and the equivalent of a character output device to our repertoire. Then, in Chapter 9, *Putting It All Together*, we'll finally implement a "Hello, World!" program. By that time you'll be well on your way to becoming an expert in the field of embedded systems programming.

Das Blinkenlights

Every embedded system that I've encountered in my career has had at least one LED that could be controlled by software. So my substitute for the "Hello, World!" program has been one that blinks an LED at a rate of 1 Hz (one complete on-off cycle per second).* Typically, the code required to turn an LED on and off is

---

* Of course, the rate of blink is completely arbitrary. But one of the things I like about the 1 Hz rate is that it's easy to confirm with a stopwatch. Simply start the stopwatch, count off some number of blinks, and see if the number of elapsed seconds is the same as the number of blinks. Need greater accuracy? Simply count off more blinks.

limited to a few lines of C or assembly, so there is very little room for programming errors to occur. And because almost all embedded systems have LEDs, the underlying concept is extremely portable.

The superstructure of the Blinking LED program is shown below. This part of the program is hardware-independent. However, it relies on the hardware-dependent functions *toggleLed* and *delay* to change the state of the LED and handle the timing, respectively.

```
/***********************************************************************
 *
 * Function:     main()
 *
 * Description:  Blink the green LED once a second.
 *
 * Notes:        This outer loop is hardware-independent.  However,
 *               it depends on two hardware-dependent functions.
 *
 * Returns:      This routine contains an infinite loop.
 *
 ***********************************************************************/
void
main(void)
{
    while (1)
    {
        toggleLed(LED_GREEN);      /* Change the state of the LED.   */
        delay(500);                /* Pause for 500 milliseconds.    */
    }

}   /* main() */
```

toggleLed

In the case of the Arcom board, there are actually two LEDs: one red and one green. The state of each LED is controlled by a bit in a register called the Port 2 I/O Latch Register (P2LTCH, for short). This register is located within the very same chip as the CPU and takes its name from the fact that it contains the latched state of eight I/O pins found on the exterior of that chip. Collectively, these pins are known as I/O Port 2. And each of the eight bits in the P2LTCH register is associated with the voltage on one of the I/O pins. For example, bit 6 controls the voltage going to the green LED:

```
#define LED_GREEN   0x40        /* The green LED is controlled by bit 6.  */
```

By modifying this bit, it is possible to change the voltage on the external pin and, thus, the state of the green LED. As shown in Figure 2-1, when bit 6 of the P2LTCH register is 1 the LED is off; when it is 0 the LED is on.

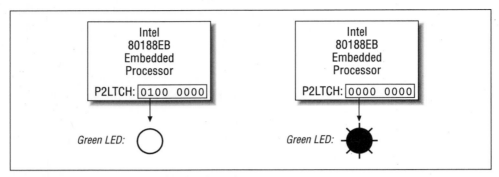

Figure 2-1. LED wiring on the Arcom board

The P2LTCH register is located in a special region of memory called the I/O space, at offset OxFF5E. Unfortunately, registers within the I/O space of an 80x86 processor can be accessed only by using the assembly language instructions in and out. The C language has no built-in support for these operations. Its closest replacements are the library routines *inport* and *outport*, which are declared in the PC-specific header file *dos.h*. Ideally, we would just include that header file and call those library routines from our embedded program. However, because they are part of the DOS programmer's library, we'll have to assume the worst: that they won't work on our system. At the very least, we shouldn't rely on them in our very first program.

An implementation of the *toggleLed* routine that is specific to the Arcom board and does not rely on any library routines is shown below. The actual algorithm is straightforward: read the contents of the P2LTCH register, toggle the bit that controls the LED of interest, and write the new value back into the register. You will notice that although this routine is written in C, the functional part is actually implemented in assembly language. This is a handy technique, known as inline assembly, that separates the programmer from the intricacies of C's function calling and parameter passing conventions but still gives her the full expressive power of assembly language.*

```
    #define P2LTCH        OxFF5E        /* The offset of the P2LTCH register. */

    /****************************************************************************
     *
     * Function:      toggleLed()
     *
     * Description: Toggle the state of one or both LEDs.
     *
```

---

* Unfortunately, the exact syntax of inline assembly varies from compiler to compiler. In the example, I'm using the format preferred by the Borland C++ compiler. Borland's inline assembly format is one of the best because it supports references to variables and constants that are defined within the C code.

```
 * Notes:         This function is specific to Arcom's Target188EB board.
 *
 * Returns:       None defined.
 *
 *****************************************************************/
void
toggleLed(unsigned char ledMask)
{
    asm {
        mov dx, P2LTCH          /* Load the address of the register.  */
        in  al, dx              /* Read the contents of the register. */

        mov ah, ledMask         /* Move the ledMask into a register.  */
        xor al, ah              /* Toggle the requested bits.         */

        out dx, al              /* Write the new register contents.   */
    };

}   /* toggleLed() */
```

delay

We also need to implement a half-second (500 ms) delay between LED toggles. This is done by busy-waiting within the *delay* routine shown below. This routine accepts the length of the requested delay, in milliseconds, as its only parameter. It then multiplies that number by the constant CYCLES_PER_MS to obtain the total number of while-loop iterations required to delay for the requested time period.

```
/*****************************************************************
 *
 * Function:    delay()
 *
 * Description: Busy-wait for the requested number of milliseconds.
 *
 * Notes:       The number of decrement-and-test cycles per millisecond
 *              was determined through trial and error.  This value is
 *              dependent upon the processor type and speed.
 *
 * Returns:     None defined.
 *
 *****************************************************************/
void
delay(unsigned int nMilliseconds)
{
    #define CYCLES_PER_MS 260 /* Number of decrement-and-test cycles. */

    unsigned long nCycles = nMilliseconds * CYCLES_PER_MS;

    while (nCycles--);

}   /* delay() */
```

The hardware-specific constant CYCLES_PER_MS represents the number of decrement-and-test cycles (nCycles-- != 0) that the processor can perform in a single millisecond. To determine this number I used trial and error. I made an approximate calculation (I think it came out to around 200), then wrote the remainder of the program, compiled it, and ran it. The LED was indeed blinking but at a rate faster than 1 Hz. So I used my trusty stopwatch to make a series of small changes to CYCLES_PER_MS until the rate of blink was as close to 1 Hz as I cared to test.

That's it! That's all there is to the Blinking LED program. The three functions *main*, *toggleLed*, and *delay* do the whole job. If you want to port this program to some other embedded system, you should read the documentation that came with your hardware, rewrite *toggleLed* as necessary, and change the value of CYCLES_PER_MS. Of course, we do still need to talk about how to build and execute this program. We'll examine those topics in the next two chapters. But first, I have a little something to say about infinite loops and their role in embedded systems.

The Role of the Infinite Loop

One of the most fundamental differences between programs developed for embedded systems and those written for other computer platforms is that the embedded programs almost always end with an infinite loop. Typically, this loop surrounds a significant part of the program's functionality—as it does in the Blinking LED program. The infinite loop is necessary because the embedded software's job is never done. It is intended to be run until either the world comes to an end or the board is reset, whichever happens first.

In addition, most embedded systems have only one piece of software running on them. And although the hardware is important, it is not a digital watch or a cellular phone or a microwave oven without that embedded software. If the software stops running, the hardware is rendered useless. So the functional parts of an embedded program are almost always surrounded by an infinite loop that ensures that they will run forever.

This behavior is so common that it's almost not worth mentioning. And I wouldn't, except that I've seen quite a few first-time embedded programmers get confused by this subtle difference. So if your first program appears to run, but instead of blinking the LED simply changes its state once, it could be that you forgot to wrap the calls to *toggleLed* and *delay* in an infinite loop.

In this chapter:
- *The Build Process*
- *Compiling*
- *Linking*
- *Locating*
- *Building das Blinkenlights*

3

Compiling, Linking, and Locating

I consider that the golden rule requires that if I like a program I must share it with other people who like it. Software sellers want to divide the users and conquer them, making each user agree not to share with others. I refuse to break solidarity with other users in this way. I cannot in good conscience sign a nondisclosure agreement or a software license agreement. So that I can continue to use computers without dishonor, I have decided to put together a sufficient body of free software so that I will be able to get along without any software that is not free.

—Richard Stallman, Founder of the GNU Project
The GNU Manifesto

In this chapter, we'll examine the steps involved in preparing your software for execution on an embedded system. We'll also discuss the associated development tools and see how to build the Blinking LED program shown in Chapter 2, *Your First Embedded Program*. But before we get started, I want to make it clear that embedded systems programming is not substantially different from the programming you've done before. The only thing that has really changed is that each target hardware platform is unique. Unfortunately, that one difference leads to a lot of additional software complexity, and it's also the reason you'll need to be more aware of the software build process than ever before.

The Build Process

There are a lot of things that software development tools can do automatically when the target platform is well defined.* This automation is possible because the tools can exploit features of the hardware and operating system on which your

---

* Used this way, the term "target platform" is best understood to include not only the hardware but also the operating system that forms the basic runtime environment for your software. If no operating system is present—as is sometimes the case in an embedded system—the target platform is simply the processor on which your program will be run.

program will execute. For example, if all of your programs will be executed on IBM-compatible PCs running DOS, your compiler can automate—and, therefore, hide from your view—certain aspects of the software build process. Embedded software development tools, on the other hand, can rarely make assumptions about the target platform. Instead, the user must provide some of his own knowledge of the system to the tools by giving them more explicit instructions.

The process of converting the source code representation of your embedded software into an executable binary image involves three distinct steps. First, each of the source files must be compiled or assembled into an object file. Second, all of the object files that result from the first step must be linked together to produce a single object file, called the relocatable program. Finally, physical memory addresses must be assigned to the relative offsets within the relocatable program in a process called relocation. The result of this third step is a file that contains an executable binary image that is ready to be run on the embedded system.

The embedded software development process just described is illustrated in Figure 3-1. In this figure, the three steps are shown from top to bottom, with the tools that perform them shown in boxes that have rounded corners. Each of these development tools takes one or more files as input and produces a single output file. More specific information about these tools and the files they produce is provided in the sections that follow.

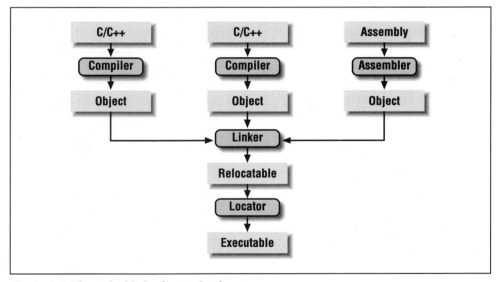

Figure 3-1. The embedded software development process

Each of the steps of the embedded software build process is a transformation performed by software running on a general-purpose computer. To distinguish this development computer (usually a PC or Unix workstation) from the target embedded system, it is referred to as the host computer. In other words, the compiler, assembler, linker, and locator are all pieces of software that run on a host computer, rather than on the embedded system itself. Yet, despite the fact that they run on some other computer platform, these tools combine their efforts to produce an executable binary image that will execute properly only on the target embedded system. This split of responsibilities is shown in Figure 3-2.

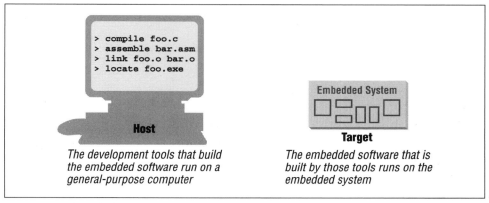

Figure 3-2. The split between host and target

In this chapter and the next I'll be using the GNU tools (compiler, assembler, linker, and debugger) as examples. These tools are extremely popular with embedded software developers because they are freely available (even the source code is free) and support many of the most popular embedded processors. I will use features of these specific tools as illustrations for the general concepts discussed. Once understood, these same basic concepts can be applied to any equivalent development tool.

Compiling

The job of a compiler is mainly to translate programs written in some human-readable language into an equivalent set of opcodes for a particular processor. In that sense, an assembler is also a compiler (you might call it an "assembly language compiler") but one that performs a much simpler one-to-one translation from one line of human-readable mnemonics to the equivalent opcode. Everything in this section applies equally to compilers and assemblers. Together these tools make up the first step of the embedded software build process.

Of course, each processor has its own unique machine language, so you need to choose a compiler that is capable of producing programs for your specific target processor. In the embedded systems case, this compiler almost always runs on the host computer. It simply doesn't make sense to execute the compiler on the embedded system itself. A compiler such as this—that runs on one computer platform and produces code for another—is called a cross-compiler. The use of a cross-compiler is one of the defining features of embedded software development.

The GNU C/C++ compiler (*gcc*) and assembler (*as*) can be configured as either native compilers or cross-compilers. As cross-compilers these tools support an impressive set of host-target combinations. Table 3-1 lists some of the most popular of the supported hosts and targets. Of course, the selections of host platform and target processor are independent; these tools can be configured for any combination.

Table 3-1. Hosts and Targets Supported by the GNU Compiler

Host Platforms	Target Processors
DEC Alpha Digital Unix	AMD/Intel x86 (32-bit only)
HP 9000/700 HP-UX	Fujitsu SPARClite
IBM Power PC AIX	Hitachi H8/300, H8/300H, H8/S
IBM RS6000 AIX	Hitachi SH
SGI Iris IRIX	IBM/Motorola PowerPC
Sun SPARC Solaris	Intel i960
Sun SPARC SunOS	MIPS R3xxx, R4xx0
X86 Windows 95/NT	Mitsubishi D10V, M32R/D
X86 Red Hat Linux	Motorola 68k
	Sun SPARC, MicroSPARC
	Toshiba TX39

Regardless of the input language (C/C++, assembly, or any other), the output of the cross-compiler will be an object file. This is a specially formatted binary file that contains the set of instructions and data resulting from the language translation process. Although parts of this file contain executable code, the object file is not intended to be executed directly. In fact, the internal structure of an object file emphasizes the incompleteness of the larger program.

The contents of an object file can be thought of as a very large, flexible data structure. The structure of the file is usually defined by a standard format like the Common Object File Format (COFF) or Extended Linker Format (ELF). If you'll be using more than one compiler (i.e., you'll be writing parts of your program in different source languages), you need to make sure that each is capable of producing object files in the same format. Although many compilers (particularly those that run on Unix platforms) support standard object file formats like COFF and ELF (*gcc* supports both), there are also some others that produce object files only in proprietary formats. If you're using one of the compilers in the latter group, you might find that you need to buy all of your other development tools from the same vendor.

Most object files begin with a header that describes the sections that follow. Each of these sections contains one or more blocks of code or data that originated within the original source file. However, these blocks have been regrouped by the compiler into related sections. For example, all of the code blocks are collected into a section called text, initialized global variables (and their initial values) into a section called data, and uninitialized global variables into a section called bss.

There is also usually a symbol table somewhere in the object file that contains the names and locations of all the variables and functions referenced within the source file. Parts of this table may be incomplete, however, because not all of the variables and functions are always defined in the same file. These are the symbols that refer to variables and functions defined in other source files. And it is up to the linker to resolve such unresolved references.

Linking

All of the object files resulting from step one must be combined in a special way before the program can be executed. The object files themselves are individually incomplete, most notably in that some of the internal variable and function references have not yet been resolved. The job of the linker is to combine these object files and, in the process, to resolve all of the unresolved symbols.

The output of the linker is a new object file that contains all of the code and data from the input object files and is in the same object file format. It does this by merging the text, data, and bss sections of the input files. So, when the linker is finished executing, all of the machine language code from all of the input object files will be in the text section of the new file, and all of the initialized and uninitialized variables will reside in the new data and bss sections, respectively.

While the linker is in the process of merging the section contents, it is also on the lookout for unresolved symbols. For example, if one object file contains an unresolved reference to a variable named foo and a variable with that same name is declared in one of the other object files, the linker will match them up. The unresolved reference will be replaced with a reference to the actual variable. In other words, if foo is located at offset 14 of the output data section, its entry in the symbol table will now contain that address.

The GNU linker (*ld*) runs on all of the same host platforms as the GNU compiler. It is essentially a command-line tool that takes the names of all the object files to be linked together as arguments. For embedded development, a special object file that contains the compiled startup code must also be included within this list. (See the sidebar "Startup Code" later in this chapter.) The GNU linker also has a scripting language that can be used to exercise tighter control over the object file that is output.

Startup Code

One of the things that traditional software development tools do automatically is to insert startup code. Startup code is a small block of assembly language code that prepares the way for the execution of software written in a high-level language. Each high-level language has its own set of expectations about the runtime environment. For example, C and C++ both utilize an implicit stack. Space for the stack has to be allocated and initialized before software written in either language can be properly executed. That is just one of the responsibilities assigned to startup code for C/C++ programs.

Most cross-compilers for embedded systems include an assembly language file called *startup.asm, crt0.s* (short for C runtime), or something similar. The location and contents of this file are usually described in the documentation supplied with the compiler.

Startup code for C/C++ programs usually consists of the following actions, performed in the order described:

1. Disable all interrupts.
2. Copy any initialized data from ROM to RAM.
3. Zero the uninitialized data area.
4. Allocate space for and initialize the stack.
5. Initialize the processor's stack pointer.
6. Create and initialize the heap.
7. Execute the constructors and initializers for all global variables (C++ only).
8. Enable interrupts.
9. Call *main.*

Typically, the startup code will also include a few instructions after the call to *main.* These instructions will be executed only in the event that the high-level language program exits (i.e., the call to *main* returns). Depending on the nature of the embedded system, you might want to use these instructions to halt the processor, reset the entire system, or transfer control to a debugging tool.

Because the startup code is not inserted automatically, the programmer must usually assemble it himself and include the resulting object file among the list of input files to the linker. He might even need to give the linker a special command-line option to prevent it from inserting the usual startup code. Working startup code for a variety of target processors can be found in a GNU package called *libgloss.*

If the same symbol is declared in more than one object file, the linker is unable to proceed. It will likely appeal to the programmer—by displaying an error message—and exit. However, if a symbol reference instead remains unresolved after all of the object files have been merged, the linker will try to resolve the reference on its own. The reference might be to a function that is part of the standard library, so the linker will open each of the libraries described to it on the command line (in the order provided) and examine their symbol tables. If it finds a function with that name, the reference will be resolved by including the associated code and data sections within the output object file.*

Unfortunately, the standard library routines often require some changes before they can be used in an embedded program. The problem here is that the standard libraries provided with most software development tool suites arrive only in object form. So you only rarely have access to the library source code to make the necessary changes yourself. Thankfully, a company called Cygnus has created a freeware version of the standard C library for use in embedded systems. This package is called *newlib*. You need only download the source code for this library from the Cygnus web site, implement a few target-specific functions, and compile the whole lot. The library can then be linked with your embedded software to resolve any previously unresolved standard library calls.

After merging all of the code and data sections and resolving all of the symbol references, the linker produces a special "relocatable" copy of the program. In other words, the program is complete except for one thing: no memory addresses have yet been assigned to the code and data sections within. If you weren't working on an embedded system, you'd be finished building your software now.

But embedded programmers aren't generally finished with the build process at this point. Even if your embedded system includes an operating system, you'll probably still need an absolutely located binary image. In fact, if there is an operating system, the code and data of which it consists are most likely within the relocatable program too. The entire embedded application—including the operating system—is almost always statically linked together and executed as a single binary image.

Locating

The tool that performs the conversion from relocatable program to executable binary image is called a locator. It takes responsibility for the easiest step of the three. In fact, you will have to do most of the work in this step yourself, by

---

* Beware that I am only talking about static linking here. In non-embedded environments, dynamic linking of libraries is very common. In that case, the code and data associated with the library routine are not inserted into the program directly.

providing information about the memory on the target board as input to the locator. The locator will use this information to assign physical memory addresses to each of the code and data sections within the relocatable program. It will then produce an output file that contains a binary memory image that can be loaded into the target ROM.

In many cases, the locator is a separate development tool. However, in the case of the GNU tools, this functionality is built right into the linker. Try not to be confused by this one particular implementation. Whether you are writing software for a general-purpose computer or an embedded system, at some point the sections of your relocatable program must have actual addresses assigned to them. In the first case, the operating system does it for you at load time. In the second, you must perform the step with a special tool. This is true even if the locator is a part of the linker, as it is in the case of *ld*.

The memory information required by the GNU linker can be passed to it in the form of a linker script. Such scripts are sometimes used to control the exact order of the code and data sections within the relocatable program. But here, we want to do more than just control the order; we also want to establish the location of each section in memory.

What follows is an example of a linker script for a hypothetical embedded target that has 512 KB each of RAM and ROM:

```
MEMORY
{
    ram : ORIGIN = 0x00000, LENGTH = 512K
    rom : ORIGIN = 0x80000, LENGTH = 512K
}

SECTIONS
{
    data ram :                          /* Initialized data.        */
    {
        _DataStart = . ;
        *(.data)
        _DataEnd   = . ;

    } >rom

    bss :                               /* Uninitialized data.      */
    {
        _BssStart = . ;
        *(.bss)
        _BssEnd   = . ;
    }

    _BottomOfHeap = . ;                 /* The heap starts here.    */
    _TopOfStack = 0x80000;              /* The stack ends here.     */
```

```
    text rom :                    /* The actual instructions.  */
    {
        *(.text)

    }
}
```

This script informs the GNU linker's built-in locator about the memory on the target board and instructs it to locate the **data** and **bss** sections in RAM (starting at address 0x00000) and the **text** section in ROM (starting at 0x80000). However, the initial values of the variables in the **data** segment will be made a part of the ROM image by the addition of **>rom** at the end of that section's definition.

All of the names that begin with underscores (**_TopOfStack**, for example) are variables that can be referenced from within your source code. The linker will use these symbols to resolve references in the input object files. So, for example, there might be a part of the embedded software (usually within the startup code) that copies the initial values of the initialized variables from ROM to the **data** section in RAM. The start and stop addresses for this operation can be established symbolically, by referring to the integer variables **_DataStart** and **_DataEnd**.

The result of this final step of the build process is an absolutely located binary image that can be downloaded to the embedded system or programmed into a read-only memory device. In the previous example, this memory image would be exactly 1 MB in size. However, because the initial values for the initialized data section are stored in ROM, the lower 512 kilobytes of this image will contain only zeros, so only the upper half of this image is significant. You'll see how to download and execute such memory images in the next chapter.

Building das Blinkenlights

Unfortunately, because we're using the Arcom board as our reference platform, we won't be able to use the GNU tools to build the examples. Instead we'll be using Borland's C++ Compiler and Turbo Assembler. These tools can be run on any DOS or Windows-based PC.* If you have an Arcom board to experiment with, this would be a good time to set it up and install the Borland development tools on your host computer. (See the appendix, *Arcom's Target188EB*, for ordering information). I used version 3.1 of the compiler, running on a Windows 95–based PC.

---

* It is interesting to note that Borland's C++ compiler was not specifically designed for use by embedded software developers. It was instead designed to produce DOS and Windows-based programs for PCs that had 80x86 processors. However, the inclusion of certain command-line options allows us to specify a particular 80x86 processor—the 80186, for example—and, thus, use this tool as a cross-compiler for embedded systems like the Arcom board.

However, any version of the Borland tools that can produce code for the 80186 processor will do.

As I have implemented it, the Blinking LED example consists of three source modules: *led.c* and *blink.c*. The first step in the build process is to compile these two files. The command-line options we'll need are *–c* for "compile, but don't link," *–v* for "include symbolic debugging information in the output," *–ml* for "use the large memory model," and *–1* for "the target is an 80186 processor." Here are the actual commands:

```
bcc -c -v -ml -1 led.c
bcc -c -v -ml -1 blink.c
```

Of course, these commands will work only if the *bcc.exe* program is in your PATH and the two source files are in the current directory. In other words, you should be in the *Chapter2* subdirectory. The result of each of these commands is the creation of an object file that has the same prefix as the *.c* file and the extension *.obj*. So if all goes well, there will now be two additional files—*led.obj* and *blink.obj*—in the working directory.

Although it would appear that there are only these two object files to be linked together in our example, there are actually three. That's because we must also include some startup code for the C program. (See the sidebar "Startup Code" earlier in this chapter.) Example startup code for the Arcom board is provided in the file *startup.asm*, which is included in the *Chapter3* subdirectory. To assemble this code into an object file, change to that directory and issue the following command:

```
tasm /mx startup.asm
```

The result should be the file *startup.obj* in that directory. The command that's actually used to link the three object files together is shown here. Beware that the order of the object files on the command line does matter in this case: the startup code must be placed first for proper linkage.

```
tlink /m /v /s ..\Chapter3\startup.obj led.obj blink.obj,
    blink.exe, blink.map
```

As a result of the *tlink* command, Borland's Turbo Linker will produce two new files: *blink.exe* and *blink.map* in the working directory. The first file contains the relocatable program and the second contains a human-readable program map. If you have never seen such a map file before, be sure to take a look at this one before reading on. It provides information similar to the contents of the linker script described earlier. However, these are results and, therefore, include the lengths of the sections and the names and locations of the public symbols found in the relocatable program.

One more tool must be used to make the Blinking LED program executable: a locator. The locating tool we'll be using is provided by Arcom, as part of the SourceVIEW development and debugging package included with the board. Because this tool is designed for this one particular embedded platform, it does not have as many options as a more general locator.* In fact, there are just three parameters: the name of the relocatable binary image, the starting address of the ROM (in hexadecimal) and the total size of the destination RAM (in kilobytes):

```
tcrom blink.exe C000 128
SourceVIEW Borland C ROM Relocator v1.06
Copyright (c) Arcom Control Systems Ltd 1994
Relocating code to ROM segment C000H, data to RAM segment 100H
Changing target RAM size to 128 Kbytes
Opening  'blink.exe'...
   Startup stack at 0102:0402
   PSP Program size     550H bytes (2K)
   Target RAM  size  20000H bytes (128K)
   Target data size     20H bytes (1K)
Creating 'blink.rom'...
   ROM  image  size     550H bytes (2K)
```

The `tcrom` locator massages the contents of the relocatable input file—assigning base addresses to each section—and outputs the file *blink.rom*. This file contains an absolutely located binary image that is ready to be loaded directly into ROM. But rather than load it into the ROM with a device programmer, we'll create a special ASCII version of the binary image that can be downloaded to the ROM over a serial port. For this we will use a utility provided by Arcom, called `bin2hex`. Here is the syntax of the command:

```
bin2hex blink.rom /A=1000
```

This extra step creates a new file, called *blink.hex*, that contains exactly the same information as *blink.rom*, but in an ASCII representation called Intel Hex Format.

---

* However, being free, it is also a lot cheaper than a more general locator.

4

In this chapter:
- When in ROM...
- Remote Debuggers
- Emulators
- Simulators and Other Tools

Downloading and Debugging

I can remember the exact instant when I realized that a large part of my life from then on was going to be spent in finding mistakes in my own programs.

—Maurice Wilkes, Head of the Computer Laboratory of the University of Cambridge, 1949

Once you have an executable binary image stored as a file on the host computer, you will need a way to download that image to the embedded system and execute it. The executable binary image is usually loaded into a memory device on the target board and executed from there. And if you have the right tools at your disposal, it will be possible to set breakpoints in the program or to observe its execution in less intrusive ways. This chapter describes various techniques for downloading, executing, and debugging embedded software.

When in ROM...

One of the most obvious ways to download your embedded software is to load the binary image into a read-only memory device and insert that chip into a socket on the target board. Obviously, the contents of a truly read-only memory device could not be overwritten. However, as you'll see in Chapter 6, *Memory*, embedded systems commonly employ special read-only memory devices that can be programmed (or reprogrammed) with the help of a special piece of equipment called a device programmer. A device programmer is a computer system that has several memory sockets on the top—of varying shapes and sizes—and is capable of programming memory devices of all sorts.

In an ideal development scenario, the device programmer would be connected to the same network as the host computer. That way, files that contain executable binary images could be easily transferred to it for ROM programming. After the binary image has been transferred to the device programmer, the memory chip is placed into the appropriately sized and shaped socket and the device type is selected from an on-screen menu. The actual device programming process can take anywhere from a few seconds to several minutes, depending on the size of the binary image and the type of memory device you are using.

After you program the ROM, it is ready to be inserted into its socket on the board. Of course, this shouldn't be done while the embedded system is still powered on. The power should be turned off and then reapplied only after the chip has been carefully inserted.

As soon as power is applied to it, the processor will begin to fetch and execute the code that is stored inside the ROM. However, beware that each type of processor has its own rules about the location of its first instruction. For example, when the Intel 80188EB processor is reset, it begins by fetching and executing whatever is stored at physical address FFFF0h. This is called the reset address, and the instructions located there are collectively known as the reset code.

If your program doesn't appear to be working, it could be there is something wrong with your reset code. You must always ensure that the binary image you've loaded into the ROM satisfies the target processor's reset rules. During product development, I often find it useful to turn on one of the board's LEDs just after the reset code has been completed. That way, I know at a glance that my new ROM either does or doesn't satisfy the processor's most basic requirements.

Debugging Tip #1: One of the most primitive debugging techniques available is the use of an LED as indicator of success or failure. The basic idea is to slowly walk the LED enable code through the larger program. In other words, you first begin with the LED enable code at the reset address. If the LED turns on, then you can edit the program, moving the LED enable code to just after the next execution milestone, rebuild, and test. This works best for very simple, linearly executed programs like the startup code. But if you don't have access to a remote debugger or any of the other debugging tools described later in this chapter, this type of debugging might be your only choice.

The Arcom board includes a special in-circuit programmable memory, called Flash memory, that does not have to be removed from the board to be reprogrammed. In fact, software that can perform the device programming function is already installed in another memory device on the board. You see, the Arcom board actually has two read-only memory devices—one (a true ROM) contains a simple program that allows the user to in-circuit program the other (a Flash memory device).

All the host computer needs to talk to the monitor program is a serial port and a terminal program. Instructions for loading an Intel Hex Format file, like *blink.hex*, into the Flash memory device are provided in the "Target188EB Monitor User's Manual," which is included with the board.

The biggest disadvantage of this download technique is that there is no easy way to debug software that is executing out of ROM. The processor fetches and executes the instructions at a high rate of speed and provides no way for you to view the internal state of the program. This might be fine once you know that your software works and you're ready to deploy the system, but it's not very helpful during software development. Of course, you can still examine the state of the LEDs and other externally visible hardware but this will never provide as much information and feedback as a debugger.

Remote Debuggers

If available, a remote debugger can be used to download, execute, and debug embedded software over a serial port or network connection between the host and target. The frontend of a remote debugger looks just like any other debugger that you might have used. It usually has a text or GUI-based main window and several smaller windows for the source code, register contents, and other relevant information about the executing program. However, in the case of embedded systems, the debugger and the software being debugged are executing on two different computer systems.

A remote debugger actually consists of two pieces of software. The frontend runs on the host computer and provides the human interface just described. But there is also a hidden backend that runs on the target processor and communicates with the frontend over a communications link of some sort. The backend provides for low-level control of the target processor and is usually called the debug monitor. Figure 4-1 shows how these two components work together.

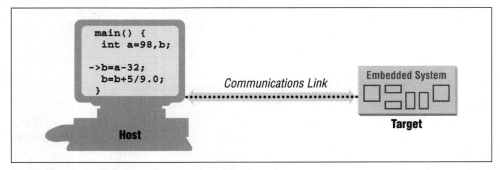

Figure 4-1. A remote debugging session

The debug monitor resides in ROM—having been placed there in the manner described earlier (either by you or at the factory)—and is automatically started whenever the target processor is reset. It monitors the communications link to the host computer and responds to requests from the remote debugger running there. Of course, these requests and the monitor's responses must conform to some predefined communications protocol and are typically of a very low-level nature. Examples of requests the remote debugger can make are "read register x," "modify register y," "read n bytes of memory starting at *address*," and "modify the data at *address*." The remote debugger combines sequences of these low-level commands to accomplish high-level debugging tasks like downloading a program, single-stepping through it, and setting breakpoints.

One such debugger is the GNU debugger (*gdb*). Like the other GNU tools, it was originally designed for use as a native debugger and was later given the ability to perform cross-platform debugging. So you can build a version of the GDB frontend that runs on any supported host and yet understands the opcodes and register names of any supported target. Source code for a compatible debug monitor is included within the GDB package and must be ported to the target platform. However, beware that this port can be tricky, particularly if you only have LED debugging at your disposal (see Debugging Tip #1).

Communication between the GDB frontend and the debug monitor is byte-oriented and designed for transmission over a serial connection. The command format and some of the major commands are shown in Table 4-1. These commands exemplify the type of interactions that occur between the typical remote debugger frontend and the debug monitor.

Table 4-1. GDB Debug Monitor Commands

Command	Request Format	Response Format
Read registers	g	*data*
Write registers	G*data*	OK
Read data at address	m*address,length*	*data*
Write data at address	M*address,length:data*	OK
Start/restart execution	c	S*signal*
Start execution from address	c*address*	S*signal*
Single step	s	S*signal*
Single step from address	s*address*	S*signal*
Reset/kill program	k	*no response*

Remote debuggers are one of the most commonly used downloading and testing tools during development of embedded software. This is mainly because of their low cost. Embedded software developers already have the requisite host computer.

In addition, the price of a remote debugger frontend does not add significantly to the cost of a suite of cross-development tools (compiler, linker, locator, etc.). Finally, the suppliers of remote debuggers often desire to give away the source code for their debug monitors, in order to increase the size of their installed user base.

As shipped, the Arcom board includes a free debug monitor in Flash memory. Together with host software provided by Arcom, this debug monitor can be used to download programs directly into target RAM and execute them. To do this, you can use the `tload` utility. Simply connect the SourceVIEW serial communications adapter to the target and host as instructed in the "SourceVIEW for Target188EB User's Manual" and issue the following command on the host PC:

```
tload -g blink.exe
SourceView Target Loader v1.4
Copyright (c) Arcom Control Systems Ltd 1994
Opening 'blink.exe'... download size   750H bytes (2K)
Checking COM1 (press ESC key to exit)...
Remote ident: TDR188EB version 1.02
Download successful
Sending 'GO' command to target system
```

The *–g* option tells the debug monitor to start executing the program as soon as the download is complete. So, this is the RAM equivalent of execution directly out of ROM. In this case, though, we want to start with the relocatable program. The `tload` utility will automatically locate the program for us, at the first available location in RAM.

For remote debugging purposes, Arcom's debug monitor can be used with Borland's Turbo Debugger as the frontend. Turbo Debugger can then be used to step through your C/C++ and assembly language programs, set breakpoints in them, and monitor variables, registers, and the stack as they execute.[*] Here's the command you would use to start a debugging session for the Blinking LED program:

```
tdr blink.exe
tver    -3.1
Target Debugger Version Changer v1.2
Copyright (c) Arcom Control Systems Ltd 1994
Checking COM1 (press ESC key to exit)...
Remote ident: TDR188EB version 1.02
TDR88 set for TD version 3.1

td -rp1 -rs3 blink.exe
Turbo Debugger Version 3.1 Copyright (c) 1988,92 Borland International
Waiting for handshake from remote driver (Ctrl-Break to quit)
```

---

[*] The actual interaction with Turbo Debugger is no different than if you were debugging a DOS or Windows application.

The *tdr* command is actually a batch file that invokes two other commands. The first tells the on-board debug monitor which version of Turbo Debugger you will be using, and the second actually invokes it. Both of these commands need to be issued each time you want to start a remote debugging session with the Arcom board. The *tdr.bat* batch file exists solely to combine them into a single command line. Again we use the relocatable version of the program because we will be downloading the program into RAM and executing it from there.

The debugger startup options *–rp1* and *–rs3* establish the parameters for the communications link to the debug monitor. *–rp1* means "remote-port=1" (COM1) and *–rs3* means "remote-speed=3" (38,400 baud). These are the parameters required to communicate with Arcom's debug monitor. After establishing a connection to the debug monitor, Turbo Debugger should start running. If it does not, there might be a problem with the serial link. Compare your setup of the link to the one in the SourceVIEW user's manual.

Once you're in Turbo Debugger, you will see a dialog box that says: "Program out of date on remote, send over link?" When you select "Yes," the contents of the file *blink.exe* will be downloaded to the target RAM. The debugger will then set an initial breakpoint at *main* and instruct the debug monitor to execute the program until that point is reached. So the next thing you should see is the C source code for *main*, with a cursor indicating that the embedded processor's instruction pointer is at the entry point to that routine.

Using normal Turbo Debugger commands, you can step through the program, set breakpoints, monitor the values stored in variables and registers, and do all of the other things debuggers allow. Or you can simply press the **F9** key to immediately execute the rest of the program. If you do this, you should then see the green LED on the front of the board start blinking. When you are satisfied that the program and the debugger are both working properly, press the reset switch attached to the Arcom board. This will cause the embedded processor to be reset, the LED to stop blinking, and Turbo Debugger to again respond to your commands.

Emulators

Remote debuggers are helpful for monitoring and controlling the state of embedded software, but only an in-circuit emulator (ICE) allows you to examine the state of the processor on which that program is running. In fact, an ICE actually takes the place of—or emulates—the processor on your target board. It is itself an embedded system, with its own copy of the target processor, RAM, ROM, and its own embedded software. As a result, in-circuit emulators are usually pretty expensive—often more expensive than the target hardware. But they are a powerful tool, and in a tight debugging spot nothing else will help you get the job done better.

Like a debug monitor, an emulator uses a remote debugger for its human interface. In some cases, it is even possible to use the same debugger frontend for both. But because the emulator has its own copy of the target processor it is possible to monitor and control the state of the processor in real time. This allows the emulator to support such powerful debugging features as hardware breakpoints and real-time tracing, in addition to the features provided by any debug monitor.

With a debug monitor, you can set breakpoints in your program. However, these software breakpoints are restricted to instruction fetches—the equivalent of the command "stop execution if this instruction is about to be fetched." Emulators, by contrast, also support hardware breakpoints. Hardware breakpoints allow you to stop execution in response to a wide variety of events. These events include not only instruction fetches, but also memory and I/O reads and writes, and interrupts. For example, you might set a hardware breakpoint on the event "variable foo contains 15 and register AX becomes 0."

Another useful feature of an in-circuit emulator is real-time tracing. Typically, an emulator incorporates a large block of special-purpose RAM that is dedicated to storing information about each of the processor cycles that are executed. This feature allows you to see in exactly what order things happened, so it can help you answer questions, such as, did the timer interrupt occur before or after the variable bar became 94? In addition, it is usually possible to either restrict the information that is stored or post-process the data prior to viewing it in order to cut down on the amount of trace data to be examined.

ROM Emulators

One other type of emulator is worth mentioning at this point. A ROM emulator is a device that emulates a read-only memory device. Like an ICE, it is an embedded system that connects to the target and communicates with the host. However, this time the target connection is via a ROM socket. To the embedded processor, it looks like any other read-only memory device. But to the remote debugger, it looks like a debug monitor.

ROM emulators have several advantages over debug monitors. First, no one has to port the debug monitor code to your particular target hardware. Second, the ROM emulator supplies its own serial or network connection to the host, so it is not necessary to use the target's own, usually limited, resources. And finally, the ROM emulator is a true replacement for the original ROM, so none of the target's memory is used up by the debug monitor code.

Simulators and Other Tools

Of course, many other debugging tools are available to you, including simulators, logic analyzers, and oscilloscopes. A simulator is a completely host-based program that simulates the functionality and instruction set of the target processor. The human interface is usually the same as or similar to that of the remote debugger. In fact, it might be possible to use one debugger frontend for the simulator back-end as well, as shown in Figure 4-2. Although simulators have many disadvantages, they are quite valuable in the earlier stages of a project when there is not yet any actual hardware for the programmers to experiment with.

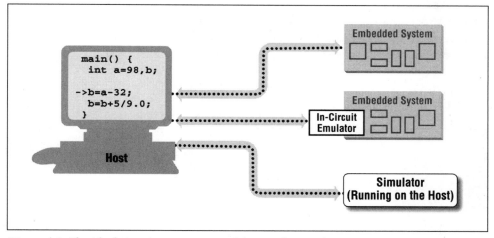

Figure 4-2. The ideal situation: a common debugger frontend

 Debugging Tip #2: If you ever encounter a situation in which the target processor is behaving differently from how you think it should from reading the data book, try running the same software in a simulator. If your program works fine there, then you know it's a hardware problem of some sort. But if the simulator exhibits the same weirdness as the actual chip, you'll know you've been misinterpreting the processor documentation all along.

By far, the biggest disadvantage of a simulator is that it only simulates the processor. And embedded systems frequently contain one or more other important peripherals. Interaction with these devices can sometimes be imitated with simulator scripts or other workarounds, but such workarounds are often more trouble to create than the simulation is valuable. So you probably won't do too much with the simulator once you have the actual embedded hardware available to you.

Once you have access to your target hardware—and especially during the hardware debugging—logic analyzers and oscilloscopes can be indispensable debugging tools. They are most useful for debugging the interactions between the processor and other chips on the board. Because they can only view signals that lie outside the processor, however, they cannot control the flow of execution of your software like a debugger or an emulator can. This makes these tools significantly less useful by themselves. But coupled with a software debugging tool like a remote debugger or an emulator, they can be extremely valuable.

A logic analyzer is a piece of laboratory equipment that is designed specifically for troubleshooting digital hardware. It can have dozens or even hundreds of inputs, each capable of detecting only one thing: whether the electrical signal it is attached to is currently at logic level 1 or 0. Any subset of the inputs that you select can be displayed against a timeline as illustrated in Figure 4-3. Most logic analyzers will also let you begin capturing data, or "trigger," on a particular pattern. For example, you might make this request: "Display the values of input signals 1 through 10, but don't start recording what happens until inputs 2 and 5 are both zero at the same time."

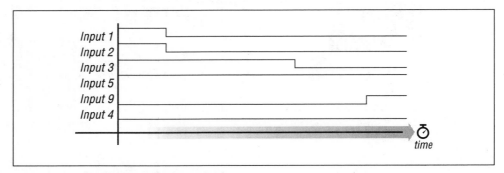

Figure 4-3. A typical logic analyzer display

 Debugging Tip #3: Occasionally it is desirable to coordinate your observation of some set of electrical signals on the target with the embedded software that is running there. For example, you might want to observe the bus interaction between the processor and one of the peripherals attached to it. A handy trick is to add an output statement to the software just prior to the start of the interaction you're interested in. This output statement should cause a unique logic pattern to appear on one or more processor pins. For example, you might cause a spare I/O pin to change from a zero to a one. The logic analyzer can then be set up to trigger on the occurrence of that event and capture everything that follows.

An oscilloscope is another piece of laboratory equipment for hardware debugging. But this one is used to examine any electrical signal, analog or digital, on any piece of hardware. Oscilloscopes are sometimes useful for quickly observing the voltage on a particular pin or, in the absence of a logic analyzer, for something slightly more complex. However, the number of inputs is much smaller (there are usually about four) and advanced triggering logic is not often available. As a result, it'll be useful to you only rarely as a software debugging tool.

Most of the debugging tools described in this chapter will be used at some point or another in every embedded project. Oscilloscopes and logic analyzers are most often used to debug hardware problems—simulators during early stages of the software development, and debug monitors and emulators during the actual software debugging. To be most effective, you should understand what each tool is for and when and where to apply it for the greatest impact.

5

Getting to Know the Hardware

In this chapter:
- *Understand the Big Picture*
- *Examine the Landscape*
- *Learn How to Communicate*
- *Get to Know the Processor*
- *Study the External Peripherals*
- *Initialize the Hardware*

> **hard·ware** n. The part of a computer system that can be kicked.

As an embedded software engineer, you'll have the opportunity to work with many different pieces of hardware in your career. In this chapter, I will teach you a simple procedure that I use to familiarize myself with any new board. In the process, I'll guide you through the creation of a header file that describes the board's most important features and a piece of software that initializes the hardware to a known state.

Understand the Big Picture

Before writing software for an embedded system, you must first be familiar with the hardware on which it will run. At first, you just need to understand the general operation of the system. You do not need to understand every little detail of the hardware; that kind of knowledge will not be needed right away and will come with time.

Whenever you receive a new board, you should take some time to read whatever documents have been provided with it. If the board is an off-the-shelf product, it might arrive with a "User's Guide" or "Programmer's Manual" that has been written with the software developer in mind. However, if the board was custom designed for your project, the documentation might be more cryptic or written mainly for the reference of the hardware designers. Either way, this is the single best place for you to start.

While you are reading the documentation, set the board itself aside. This will help you to focus on the big picture. There will be plenty of time to examine the actual board more closely when you have finished reading. Before picking up the board, you should be able to answer two basic questions about it:

- What is the overall purpose of the board?
- How does data flow through it?

For example, imagine that you are a member of a modem design team. You are a software developer who has just received an early prototype board from the hardware designers. Because you are already familiar with modems, the overall purpose of the board and the data-flow through it should be fairly obvious to you. The purpose of the board is to send and receive digital data over an analog telephone line. The hardware reads digital data from one set of electrical connections and writes an analog version of the data to an attached telephone line. Data also flows in the opposite direction, when analog data is read from the telephone line jack and output digitally.

Though the purpose of most systems is fairly obvious, the flow of the data might not be. I often find that a data-flow diagram is helpful in achieving rapid comprehension. If you are lucky, the documentation provided with your hardware will contain a superset of the block diagram you need. However, you might still find it useful to create your own data-flow diagram. That way, you can leave out those hardware components that are unrelated to the basic flow of data through the system.

In the case of the Arcom board, the hardware was not designed with a particular application in mind. So for the remainder of this chapter, we'll have to imagine that it does have a purpose. We shall assume the board was designed for use as a printer-sharing device. A printer-sharing device allows two computers to share a single printer. The user of the device connects one computer to each serial port and a printer to the parallel port. Both computers can then send documents to the printer, though only one of them can do so at a given time.

In order to illustrate the flow of data through the printer-sharing device, I've drawn the diagram in Figure 5-1. (Only those hardware devices that are involved in this application of the Arcom board are shown.) By looking at the block diagram, you should be able to quickly visualize the flow of the data through the system. Data to be printed is accepted from either serial port, held in RAM until the printer is ready for more data, and delivered to the printer via the parallel port. The software that makes all of this happen is stored in ROM.

Once you've created a block diagram, don't just crumple it up and throw it away. You should instead put it where you can refer to it throughout the project. I recommend creating a project notebook or binder, with this data-flow diagram on the first page. As you continue working with this piece of hardware, write down everything you learn about it in your notebook. You might also want to keep

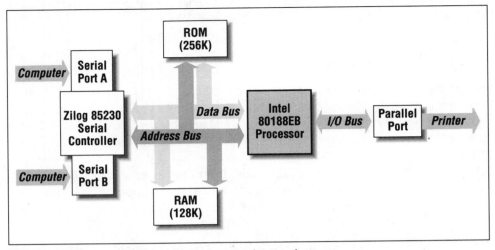

Figure 5-1. Data-flow diagram for the printer-sharing device

notes about the software design and implementation. A project notebook is valuable not only while you are developing the software, but also once the project is complete. You will appreciate the extra effort you put into keeping a notebook when you need to make changes to your software, or work with similar hardware, months or years later.

If you still have any big-picture questions after reading the hardware documents, ask a hardware engineer for some help. If you don't already know the hardware's designer, take a few minutes to introduce yourself. If you have some time, take him out to lunch or buy him a beer after work. (You don't even have to talk about the project the whole time!) I have found that many software engineers have difficulty communicating with hardware engineers, and vice versa. In embedded systems development, it is especially important that the hardware and software teams be able to communicate with one another.

Examine the Landscape

It is often useful to put yourself in the processor's shoes for a while. After all, the processor is only going to do what you ultimately instruct it to do with your software. Imagine what it is like to be the processor: what does the processor's world look like? If you think about it from this perspective, one thing you quickly realize is that the processor has a lot of compatriots. These are the other pieces of hardware on the board, with which the processor can communicate directly. In this section you will learn to recognize their names and addresses.

The first thing to notice is that there are two basic types: memories and peripherals. Obviously, memories are for data and code storage and retrieval. But you might be wondering what the peripherals are. These are specialized hardware devices that either coordinate interaction with the outside world (I/O) or perform a specific hardware function. For example, two of the most common peripherals in embedded systems are serial ports and timers. The former is an I/O device, and the latter is basically just a counter.

Members of Intel's 80x86 and some other processor families have two distinct address spaces through which they can communicate with these memories and peripherals. The first address space is called the memory space and is intended mainly for memory devices; the second is reserved exclusively for peripherals and is called the I/O space. However, peripherals can also be located within the memory space, at the discretion of the hardware designer. When that happens, we say that those peripherals are memory-mapped.

From the processor's point of view, memory-mapped peripherals look and act very much like memory devices. However, the function of a peripheral is obviously quite different from that of a memory. Instead of simply storing the data that is provided to it, a peripheral might instead interpret it as a command or as data to be processed in some way. If peripherals are located within the memory space, we say that the system has memory-mapped I/O.

The designers of embedded hardware often prefer to use memory-mapped I/O exclusively, because it has advantages for both the hardware and software developers. It is attractive to the hardware developer because he might be able to eliminate the I/O space, and some of its associated wires, altogether. This might not significantly reduce the production cost of the board, but it might reduce the complexity of the hardware design. Memory-mapped peripherals are also better for the programmer, who is able to use pointers, data structures, and unions to interact with the peripherals more easily and efficiently.[*]

Memory Map

All processors store their programs and data in memory. In some cases this memory resides on the very same chip as the processor, but more often it is located in external memory chips. These chips are located in the processor's memory space, and the processor communicates with them by way of two sets of electrical wires called the address bus and the data bus. To read or write a particular location in memory, the processor first writes the desired address onto the address bus. The data is then transferred over the data bus.

---

[*] The *toggleLed* function wouldn't have required a single line of assembly code if the P2LTCH register had been memory-mapped.

As you are reading about a new board, create a table that shows the name and address range of each memory device and peripheral that is located in the memory space. Organize the table so that the lowest address is at the bottom and the highest address is at the top. Each time you add a device to the memory map, place it in its approximate location in memory and label the starting and ending addresses, in hexadecimal. After you have finished inserting all of the devices into the memory map, be sure to label any unused memory regions as such.

If you look back at the block diagram of the Arcom board in Figure 5-1, you will see that there are three devices attached to the address and data buses. These devices are the RAM and ROM and a mysterious device labeled "Zilog 85230 Serial Controller." The documentation provided by Arcom says that the RAM is located at the bottom of memory and extends upward for the first 128 KB of the memory space. The ROM is located at the top of memory and extends downward for 256 KB. But this area of memory actually contains two ROMs—an EPROM and a Flash memory device—each of size 128 KB. The third device, the Zilog 85230 Serial Communications Controller, is a memory-mapped peripheral whose registers are accessible between the addresses 70000h and 72000h.

The memory map in Figure 5-2 shows what these devices look like to the processor. In a sense, this is the processor's "address book." Just as you maintain a list of names and addresses in your personal life, you must maintain a similar list for the processor. The memory map contains one entry for each of the memories and peripherals that are accessible from the processor's memory space. This diagram is arguably the most important piece of information about the system and should be kept up-to-date and as part of the permanent records associated with the project.

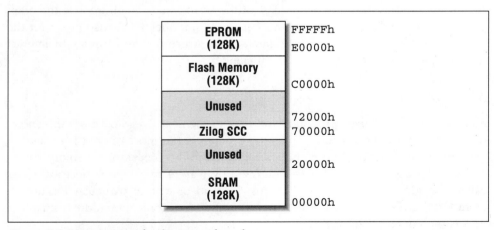

Figure 5-2. Memory map for the Arcom board

For each new board, you should create a header file that describes its most important features. This file provides an abstract interface to the hardware. In effect, it allows you to refer to the various devices on the board by name, rather than by address. This has the added benefit of making your application software more portable. If the memory map ever changes—for example, if the 128 KB of RAM is moved—you need only change the affected lines of the board-specific header file and recompile your application.

As this chapter progresses, I will show you how to create a header file for the Arcom board. The first section of this file is listed below. The part of the header file below describes the memory map. The most notable difference between the memory map in the header file and that in Figure 5-2 is the format of the addresses. The sidebar "Pointers Versus Addresses" explains why.

```
/************************************************************************
 *
 *   Memory Map
 *
 *           Base Address   Size   Description
 *           --------------  -----  -----------------------------------
 *           0000:0000h     128K   SRAM
 *           2000:0000h            Unused
 *           7000:0000h            Zilog SCC Registers
 *           7000:1000h            Zilog SCC Interrupt Acknowledge
 *           7000:2000h            Unused
 *           C000:0000h     128K   Flash
 *           E000:0000h     128K   EPROM
 *
 ************************************************************************/

#define SRAM_BASE     (void *) 0x00000000
#define SCC_BASE      (void *) 0x70000000
#define SCC_INTACK    (void *) 0x70001000
#define FLASH_BASE    (void *) 0xC0000000
#define EPROM_BASE    (void *) 0xE0000000
```

I/O Map

If a separate I/O space is present, it will be necessary to repeat the memory map exercise to create an I/O map for the board as well. The process is exactly the same. Simply create a table of peripheral names and address ranges, organized in such a way that the lowest addresses are at the bottom. Typically, a large percentage of the I/O space will be unused because most of the peripherals located there will have only a handful of registers.

The I/O map for the Arcom board is shown in Figure 5-3. It includes three devices: the peripheral control block (PCB), parallel port, and debugger port. The PCB is a set of registers within the 80188EB that are used to control the on-chip

Pointers Versus Addresses

In both C and C++, the value of a pointer is an address. So when we say that we have a pointer to some data, we really mean that we have the address at which the data is stored. But programmers don't usually set or examine these addresses directly. The exception to this rule are the developers of operating systems, device drivers, and embedded software, who sometimes need to set the value of a pointer explicitly in their code.

Unfortunately, the exact representation of an address can change from processor to processor or can even be compiler dependent. This means that a physical address like 12345h might not be stored in exactly that form, or might even be stored differently by different compilers.* The issue that then arises is how a programmer can set the value of a pointer explicitly so that it points to the desired location in the memory map.

Most C/C++ compilers for 80x86 processors use 32-bit pointers. However, the older processors don't have a simple linear 32-bit address space. For example, Intel's 80188EB processor has only a 20-bit address space. And, in addition, none of its internal registers can hold more than 16 bits. So on this processor, two 16-bit registers—a segment register and an offset register—are combined to create the 20-bit physical address. (The physical address computation involves left-shifting the contents of the segment register by four bits and adding the contents of the offset register to the result. Any overflow into the 21st bit is ignored.)

To declare and initialize a pointer to a register located at physical address 12345h we therefore write:

```
int * pRegister = (int *) 0x10002345;
```

where the leftmost 16 bits contain the segment value and the rightmost 16 bits contain the offset value.

For convenience, 80x86 programmers sometimes write addresses as segment:offset pairs. Using this notation, the physical address 12345h would be written as `0x1000:2345`. This is precisely the value—sans colon—that we used to initialize the pointer above. However, for each possible physical address there are 4096 distinct segment:offset pairs that point to a given physical address. For example, the pairs `0x1200:0345` and `0x1234:0005` (and 4093 others) also refer to physical address 12345h.

---

* This situation gets even more complicated if you consider the various memory models provided by some processors. All of the examples in this book assume that the 80188's large memory model is used. In this memory model all of the specifics I'm about to tell you hold for all pointer types. But in the other memory models, the format of the address stored in a pointer differs depending upon the type of code or data pointed to!

peripherals. The chips that control the parallel port and debugger port reside outside of the processor. These ports are used to communicate with the printer and a host-based debugger, respectively.

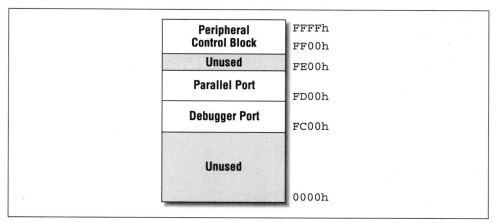

Figure 5-3. I/O map for the Arcom board

The I/O map is also useful when creating the header file for your board. Each region of the I/O space maps directly to a constant, called the base address. The translation of the above I/O map into a set of constants can be found in the following listing:

```
/*******************************************************************
 *
 *  I/O Map
 *
 *              Base Address    Description
 *              --------------- ------------------------------------
 *              0000h           Unused
 *              FC00h           SourceVIEW Debugger Port (SVIEW)
 *              FD00h           Parallel I/O Port (PIO)
 *              FE00h           Unused
 *              FF00h           Peripheral Control Block (PCB)
 *
 *******************************************************************/

#define SVIEW_BASE    0xFC00
#define PIO_BASE      0xFD00
#define PCB_BASE      0xFF00
```

Learn How to Communicate

Now that you know the names and addresses of the memory and peripherals attached to the processor, it is time to learn how to communicate with the latter.

There are two basic communication techniques: polling and interrupts. In either case, the processor usually issues some sort of commands to the device—by way of the memory or I/O space—and waits for the device to complete the assigned task. For example, the processor might ask a timer to count down from 1000 to 0. Once the countdown begins, the processor is interested in just one thing: is the timer finished counting yet?

If polling is used, then the processor repeatedly checks to see if the task has been completed. This is analogous to the small child who repeatedly asks "are we there yet?" throughout a long trip. Like the child, the processor spends a large amount of otherwise useful time asking the question and getting a negative response. To implement polling in software, you need only create a loop that reads the status register of the device in question. Here is an example:

```
do
{
    // Play games, read, listen to music, etc.
    ...

    // Poll to see if we're there yet.
    status = areWeThereYet();

} while (status == NO);
```

The second communication technique uses interrupts. An interrupt is an asynchronous electrical signal from a peripheral to the processor. When interrupts are used, the processor issues commands to the peripheral exactly as before, but then waits for an interrupt to signal completion of the assigned work. While the processor is waiting for the interrupt to arrive, it is free to continue working on other things. When the interrupt signal is finally asserted, the processor temporarily sets aside its current work and executes a small piece of software called the interrupt service routine (ISR). When the ISR completes, the processor returns to the work that was interrupted.

Of course, this isn't all automatic. The programmer must write the ISR himself and "install" and enable it so that it will be executed when the relevant interrupt occurs. The first few times you do this, it will be a significant challenge. But, even so, the use of interrupts generally decreases the complexity of one's overall code by giving it a better structure. Rather than device polling being embedded within an unrelated part of the program, the two pieces of code remain appropriately separate.

On the whole, interrupts are a much more efficient use of the processor than polling. The processor is able to use a larger percentage of its waiting time to perform useful work. However, there is some overhead associated with each interrupt. It takes a good bit of time—relative to the length of time it takes to execute an opcode—to put aside the processor's current work and transfer control to the interrupt service routine. Many of the processor's registers must be saved in memory, and lower-priority interrupts must be disabled. So in practice both methods are used frequently. Interrupts are used when efficiency is paramount or multiple devices must be monitored simultaneously. Polling is used when the processor must respond to some event more quickly than is possible using interrupts.

Interrupt Map

Most embedded systems have only a handful of interrupts. Associated with each of these are an interrupt pin (on the outside of the processor chip) and an ISR. In order for the processor to execute the correct ISR, a mapping must exist between interrupt pins and ISRs. This mapping usually takes the form of an interrupt vector table. The vector table is usually just an array of pointers to functions, located at some known memory address. The processor uses the interrupt type (a unique number associated with each interrupt pin) as its index into this array. The value stored at that location in the vector table is usually just the address of the ISR to be executed.[*]

It is important to initialize the interrupt vector table correctly. (If it is done incorrectly, the ISR might be executed in response to the wrong interrupt or never executed at all.) The first part of this process is to create an interrupt map that organizes the relevant information. An interrupt map is a table that contains a list of interrupt types and the devices to which they refer. This information should be included in the documentation provided with the board. Table 5-1 shows the interrupt map for the Arcom board.

Table 5-1. Interrupt Map for the Arcom Board

Interrupt Type	Generating Device
8	Timer/Counter #0
17	Zilog 85230 SCC
18	Timer/Counter #1
19	Timer/Counter #2
20	Serial Port Receive
21	Serial Port Transmit

Once again, our goal is to translate the information in the table into a form that is useful for the programmer. After constructing an interrupt map like the one above,

---

[*] A few processors actually have the first few instructions of the ISR stored there, rather than a pointer to the routine.

you should add a third section to the board-specific header file. Each line of the interrupt map becomes a single `#define` within the file, as shown:

```
/*************************************************************************
 *
 *   Interrupt Map
 *
 *************************************************************************/

/*
 * Zilog 85230 SCC
 */
#define SCC_INT          17

/*
 * On-Chip Timer/Counters
 */
#define TIMER0_INT        8
#define TIMER1_INT       18
#define TIMER2_INT       19

/*
 * On-Chip Serial Ports
 */
#define RX_INT           20
#define TX_INT           21
```

Get to Know the Processor

If you haven't worked with the processor on your board before, you should take some time to get familiar with it now. This shouldn't take very long if you do all of your programming in C or C++. To the user of a high-level language, most processors look and act pretty much the same. However, if you'll be doing any assembly language programming, you will need to familiarize yourself with the processor's architecture and basic instruction set.

Everything you need to know about the processor can be found in the databooks provided by the manufacturer. If you don't have a databook or programmer's guide for your processor already, you should obtain one immediately. If you are going to be a successful embedded systems programmer, you must be able to read databooks and get something out of them. Processor databooks are usually well written—as databooks go—so they are an ideal place to start. Begin by flipping through the databook and noting the sections that are most relevant to the tasks at hand. Then go back and begin reading the processor overview section.

Processors in General

Many of the most common processors are members of families of related devices. In some cases, the members of such a processor family represent points along an evolutionary path. The most obvious example is Intel's 80x86 family, which spans from the original 8086 to the Pentium II—and beyond. In fact, the 80x86 family has been so successful that it has spawned an entire industry of imitators.

As it is used in this book, the term *processor* refers to any of three types of devices known as microprocessors, microcontrollers, and digital signal processors. The name microprocessor is usually reserved for a chip that contains a powerful CPU that has not been designed with any particular computation in mind. These chips are usually the foundation of personal computers and high-end workstations. The most common microprocessors are members of Motorola's 68k—found in older Macintosh computers—and the ubiquitous 80x86 families.

A microcontroller is very much like a microprocessor, except that it has been designed specifically for use in embedded systems. Microcontrollers typically include a CPU, memory (a small amount of RAM, ROM, or both), and other peripherals in the same integrated circuit. If you purchase all of these items on a single chip, it is possible to reduce the cost of an embedded system substantially. Among the most popular microcontrollers are the 8051 and its many imitators and Motorola's 68HCxx series. It is also common to find microcontroller versions of popular microprocessors. For example, Intel's 386EX is a microcontroller version of the very successful 80386 microprocessor.

The final type of processor is a digital signal processor, or DSP. The CPU within a DSP is specially designed to perform discrete-time signal processing calculations—like those required for audio and video communications—extremely fast. Because DSPs can perform these types of calculations much faster than other processors, they offer a powerful, low-cost microprocessor alternative for designers of modems and other telecommunications and multimedia equipment. Two of the most common DSP families are the TMS320Cxx and 5600x series from TI and Motorola, respectively.

Intel's 80188EB Processor

The processor on the Arcom board is an Intel 80188EB—a microcontroller version of the 80186. In addition to the CPU, the 80188EB contains an interrupt control unit, two programmable I/O ports, three timer/counters, two serial ports, a DRAM controller, and a chip-select unit. These extra hardware devices are located within the same chip and are referred to as on-chip peripherals. The CPU is able to communicate with and control the on-chip peripherals directly, via internal buses.

Although the on-chip peripherals are distinct hardware devices, they act like little extensions of the 80186 CPU. The software can control them by reading and writing a 256-byte block of registers known as the peripheral control block (PCB). You may recall that we encountered this block when we first discussed the memory and I/O maps for the board. By default the PCB is located in the I/O space, beginning at address FF00h. However, if so desired, the PCB can be relocated to any convenient address in either the I/O or memory space.

The control and status registers for each of the on-chip peripherals are located at fixed offsets from the PCB base address. The exact offset of each register can be found in a table in the 80188EB Microprocessor User's Manual. To isolate these details from your application software, it is good practice to include the offsets of any registers you will be using in the header file for your board. I have done this for the Arcom board, but only those registers that will be discussed in later chapters of the book are shown here:

```
/*********************************************************************
 *
 *  On-Chip Peripherals
 *
 *********************************************************************/

/*
 * Interrupt Control Unit
 */
#define EOI      (PCB_BASE + 0x02)
#define POLL     (PCB_BASE + 0x04)
#define POLLSTS  (PCB_BASE + 0x06)

#define IMASK    (PCB_BASE + 0x08)
#define PRIMSK   (PCB_BASE + 0x0A)

#define INSERV   (PCB_BASE + 0x0C)
#define REQST    (PCB_BASE + 0x0E)
#define INSTS    (PCB_BASE + 0x10)

/*
 * Timer/Counters
 */
#define TCUCON   (PCB_BASE + 0x12)

#define T0CNT    (PCB_BASE + 0x30)
#define T0CMPA   (PCB_BASE + 0x32)
#define T0CMPB   (PCB_BASE + 0x34)
#define T0CON    (PCB_BASE + 0x36)

#define T1CNT    (PCB_BASE + 0x38)
#define T1CMPA   (PCB_BASE + 0x3A)
#define T1CMPB   (PCB_BASE + 0x3C)
#define T1CON    (PCB_BASE + 0x3E)

#define T2CNT    (PCB_BASE + 0x40)
#define T2CMPA   (PCB_BASE + 0x42)
#define T2CON    (PCB_BASE + 0x46)

/*
 * Programmable I/O Ports
 */
```

```
#define P1DIR    (PCB_BASE + 0x50)
#define P1PIN    (PCB_BASE + 0x52)
#define P1CON    (PCB_BASE + 0x54)
#define P1LTCH   (PCB_BASE + 0x56)

#define P2DIR    (PCB_BASE + 0x58)
#define P2PIN    (PCB_BASE + 0x5A)
#define P2CON    (PCB_BASE + 0x5C)
#define P2LTCH   (PCB_BASE + 0x5E)
```

Other things you'll want to learn about the processor from its databook are:

- Where should the interrupt vector table be located? Does it have to be located at a specific address in memory? If not, how does the processor know where to find it?

- What is the format of the interrupt vector table? Is it just a table of pointers to ISR functions?

- Are there any special interrupts, sometimes called traps, that are generated within the processor itself? Must an ISR be written to handle each of these?

- How are interrupts enabled and disabled (globally and individually)?

- How are interrupts acknowledged or cleared?

Study the External Peripherals

At this point, you've studied every aspect of the new hardware except the external peripherals. These are the hardware devices that reside outside the processor chip and communicate with it by way of interrupts and I/O or memory-mapped registers.

Begin by making a list of the external peripherals. Depending on your application, this list might include LCD or keyboard controllers, A/D converters, network interface chips, or custom ASICs (Application-Specific Generated Circuits). In the case of the Arcom board, the list contains just three items: the Zilog 85230 Serial Controller, parallel port, and debugger port.

You should obtain a copy of the user's manual or databook for each device on your list. At this early stage of the project, your goal in reading these documents is to understand the basic functions of the device. What does the device do? What registers are used to issue commands and receive the results? What do the various bits and larger fields within these registers mean? When, if ever, does the device generate interrupts? How are interrupts acknowledged or cleared at the device?

When you are designing the embedded software, you should try to break the program down along device lines. It is usually a good idea to associate a software module called a device driver with each of the external peripherals. This is nothing more than a collection of software routines that control the operation of the peripheral and isolate the application software from the details of that particular hardware device. I'll have a lot more to say about device drivers in Chapter 7, *Peripherals*.

Initialize the Hardware

The final step in getting to know your new hardware is to write some initialization software. This is your best opportunity to develop a close working relationship with the hardware—especially if you will be developing the remainder of the software in a high-level language. During hardware initialization it will be impossible to avoid using assembly language. However, after completing this step, you will be ready to begin writing small programs in C or C++.*

 If you are one of the first software engineers to work with a new board—especially a prototype—the hardware might not work as advertised. All processor-based boards require some amount of software testing to confirm the correctness of the hardware design and the proper functioning of the various peripherals. This puts you in an awkward position when something is not working properly. How do you know if the hardware or your software is to blame? If you happen to be good with hardware or have access to a simulator, you might be able to construct some experiments to answer this question. Otherwise, you should probably ask a hardware engineer to join you in the lab for a joint debugging session.

The hardware initialization should be executed before the startup code described in Chapter 3, *Compiling, Linking, and Locating*. The code described there assumes that the hardware has already been initialized and concerns itself only with creating a proper runtime environment for high-level language programs. Figure 5-4 provides an overview of the entire initialization process, from processor reset through hardware initialization and C/C++ startup code to *main*.

The first stage of the initialization process is the reset code. This is a small piece of assembly (usually only two or three instructions) that the processor executes immediately after it is powered on or reset. The sole purpose of this code is to transfer control to the hardware initialization routine. The first instruction of the reset code must be placed at a specific location in memory, usually called the reset

---

* In order to make the example in Chapter 2, *Your First Embedded Program*, a little easier to understand, I didn't show any of the initialization code there. However, it is necessary to get the hardware initialization code working before you can write even simple programs like Blinking LED.

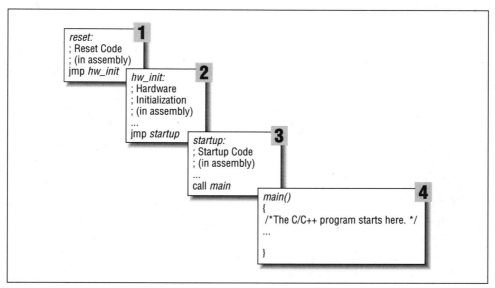

Figure 5-4: The hardware and software initialization process

address, that is specified in the processor databook. The reset address for the 80188EB is FFFF0h.

Most of the actual hardware initialization takes place in the second stage. At this point, we need to inform the processor about its environment. This is also a good place to initialize the interrupt controller and other critical peripherals. Less critical hardware devices can be initialized when the associated device driver is started, usually from within *main.*

Intel's 80188EB has several internal registers that must be programmed before any useful work can be done with the processor. These registers are responsible for setting up the memory and I/O maps and are part of the processor's internal chip-select unit. By programming the chip-select registers, you are essentially waking up each of the memory and I/O devices that are connected to the processor. Each chip-select register is associated with a single "chip enable" wire that runs from the processor to some other chip. The association between particular chip-selects and hardware devices must be established by the hardware designer. All you need to do is get a list of chip-select settings from him and load those settings into the chip-select registers.

Upon reset, the 80188EB assumes a worst-case scenario. It assumes there are only 1024 bytes of ROM—located in the address range FFC00h to FFFFFh—and that no other memory or I/O devices are present. This is the processor's "fetal position," and it implies that the *hw_init* routine must be located at address FFC00h (or higher). It must also not require the use of any RAM. The hardware initialization routine should start by initializing the chip-select registers to inform the processor about the other memory and I/O devices that are installed on the board. By the time this task is complete, the entire range of ROM and RAM addresses will be enabled, so the remainder of your software can be located at any convenient address in either ROM or RAM.

The third initialization stage contains the startup code. This is the assembly-language code that we saw back in Chapter 3. In case you don't remember, its job is to the prepare the way for code written in a high-level language. Of importance here is only that the startup code calls *main*. From that point forward, all of your other software can be written in C or C++.

Hopefully, you are starting to understand how embedded software gets from processor reset to your main program. Admittedly, the very first time you try to pull all of these components together (reset code, hardware initialization, C/C++ startup code, and application) on a new board there will be problems. So expect to spend some time debugging each of them. Honestly, this will be the hardest part of the project. You will soon see that once you have a working Blinking LED program to fall back on, the work just gets easier and easier—or at least more similar to ordinary computer programming.

Up to this point in the book we have been building the infrastructure for embedded programming. But the topics we're going to talk about in the remaining chapters concern higher-level structures: memory tests, device drivers, operating systems, and actually useful programs. These are pieces of software you've probably seen before on other computer systems projects. However, there will still be some new twists related to the embedded programming environment.

In this chapter:
- *Types of Memory*
- *Memory Testing*
- *Validating Memory Contents*
- *Working with Flash Memory*

6

Memory

> *Tyrell: If we give them a past, we create a cushion for their emotions and, consequently, we can control them better.*
>
> *Deckard: Memories. You're talking about memories.*
>
> — the movie *Blade Runner*

In this chapter, you will learn everything you need to know about memory in embedded systems. In particular, you will learn about the types of memory you are likely to encounter, how to test memory devices to see if they are working properly, and how to use Flash memory.

Types of Memory

Many types of memory devices are available for use in modern computer systems. As an embedded software engineer, you must be aware of the differences between them and understand how to use each type effectively. In our discussion, we will approach these devices from a software viewpoint. As you are reading, try to keep in mind that the development of these devices took several decades and that there are significant physical differences in the underlying hardware. The names of the memory types frequently reflect the historical nature of the development process and are often more confusing than insightful.

Most software developers think of memory as being either random-access (RAM) or read-only (ROM). But, in fact, there are subtypes of each and even a third class of hybrid memories. In a RAM device, the data stored at each memory location can be read or written, as desired. In a ROM device, the data stored at each memory location can be read at will, but never written. In some cases, it is possible to overwrite the data in a ROM-like device. Such devices are called hybrid memories because they exhibit some of the characteristics of both RAM and ROM. Figure 6-1 provides a classification system for the memory devices that are commonly found in embedded systems.

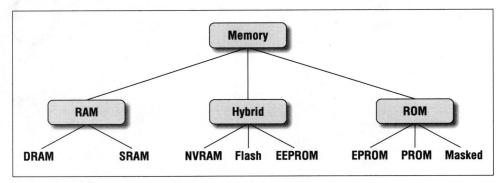

Figure 6-1. Common memory types in embedded systems

Types of RAM

There are two important memory devices in the RAM family: SRAM and DRAM. The main difference between them is the lifetime of the data stored. SRAM (static RAM) retains its contents as long as electrical power is applied to the chip. However, if the power is turned off or lost temporarily then its contents will be lost forever. DRAM (dynamic RAM), on the other hand, has an extremely short data lifetime—usually less than a quarter of a second. This is true even when power is applied constantly.

In short, SRAM has all the properties of the memory you think of when you hear the word RAM. Compared to that, DRAM sounds kind of useless. What good is a memory device that retains its contents for only a fraction of a second? By itself, such a volatile memory is indeed worthless. However, a simple piece of hardware called a DRAM controller can be used to make DRAM behave more like SRAM. (See the sidebar "DRAM Controllers" later in this chapter.) The job of the DRAM controller is to periodically refresh the data stored in the DRAM. By refreshing the data several times a second, the DRAM controller keeps the contents of memory alive for as long as they are needed. So, DRAM is as useful as SRAM after all.

When deciding which type of RAM to use, a system designer must consider access time and cost. SRAM devices offer extremely fast access times (approximately four times faster than DRAM) but are much more expensive to produce. Generally, SRAM is used only where access speed is extremely important. A lower cost per byte makes DRAM attractive whenever large amounts of RAM are required. Many embedded systems include both types: a small block of SRAM (a few hundred kilobytes) along a critical data path and a much larger block of DRAM (in the megabytes) for everything else.

DRAM Controllers

If your embedded system includes DRAM, there is probably a DRAM controller on board (or on-chip) as well. The DRAM controller is an extra piece of hardware placed between the processor and the memory chips. Its main purpose is to perform the refresh operations required to keep your data alive in the DRAM. However, it cannot do this properly without some help from you.

One of the first things your software must do is initialize the DRAM controller. If you do not have any other RAM in the system, you must do this before creating the stack or heap. As a result, this initialization code is usually written in assembly language and placed within the hardware initialization module.

Almost all DRAM controllers require a short initialization sequence that consists of one or more setup commands. The setup commands tell the controller about the hardware interface to the DRAM and how frequently the data there must be refreshed. To determine the initialization sequence for your particular system, consult the designer of the board or read the databooks that describe the DRAM and DRAM controller. If the DRAM in your system does not appear to be working properly, it could be that the DRAM controller either is not initialized or has been initialized incorrectly.

Types of ROM

Memories in the ROM family are distinguished by the methods used to write new data to them (usually called programming) and the number of times they can be rewritten. This classification reflects the evolution of ROM devices from hardwired to one-time programmable to erasable-and-programmable. A common feature across all these devices is their ability to retain data and programs forever, even during a power failure.

The very first ROMs were hardwired devices that contained a preprogrammed set of data or instructions. The contents of the ROM had to be specified before chip production, so the actual data could be used to arrange the transistors inside the chip! Hardwired memories are still used, though they are now called "masked ROMs" to distinguish them from other types of ROM. The main advantage of a masked ROM is a low production cost. Unfortunately, the cost is low only when hundreds of thousands of copies of the same ROM are required.

One step up from the masked ROM is the PROM (programmable ROM), which is purchased in an unprogrammed state. If you were to look at the contents of an unprogrammed PROM, you would see that the data is made up entirely of 1's. The process of writing your data to the PROM involves a special piece of equipment called a device programmer. The device programmer writes data to the device one word at a time, by applying an electrical charge to the input pins of the chip. Once a PROM has been programmed in this way, its contents can never be changed. If the code or data stored in the PROM must be changed, the current device must be discarded. As a result, PROMs are also known as *one-time programmable* (OTP) devices.

An EPROM (erasable-and-programmable ROM) is programmed in exactly the same manner as a PROM. However, EPROMs can be erased and reprogrammed repeatedly. To erase an EPROM, you simply expose the device to a strong source of ultraviolet light. (There is a "window" in the top of the device to let the ultraviolet light reach the silicon.) By doing this, you essentially reset the entire chip to its initial—unprogrammed—state. Though more expensive than PROMs, their ability to be reprogrammed makes EPROMs an essential part of the software development and testing process.

Hybrid Types

As memory technology has matured in recent years, the line between RAM and ROM devices has blurred. There are now several types of memory that combine the best features of both. These devices do not belong to either group and can be collectively referred to as hybrid memory devices. Hybrid memories can be read and written as desired, like RAM, but maintain their contents without electrical power, just like ROM. Two of the hybrid devices, EEPROM and Flash, are descendants of ROM devices; the third, NVRAM, is a modified version of SRAM.

EEPROMs are electrically-erasable-and-programmable. Internally, they are similar to EPROMs, but the erase operation is accomplished electrically, rather than by exposure to ultraviolet light. Any byte within an EEPROM can be erased and rewritten. Once written, the new data will remain in the device forever—or at least until it is electrically erased. The tradeoff for this improved functionality is mainly higher cost. Write cycles are also significantly longer than writes to a RAM, so you wouldn't want to use an EEPROM for your main system memory.

Flash memory is the most recent advancement in memory technology. It combines all the best features of the memory devices described thus far. Flash memory devices are high density, low cost, nonvolatile, fast (to read, but not to write), and electrically reprogrammable. These advantages are overwhelming and the use of Flash memory has increased dramatically in embedded systems as a direct result. From a software viewpoint, Flash and EEPROM technologies are very similar. The major difference is that Flash devices can be erased only one sector at a time, not byte by byte. Typical sector sizes are in the range of 256 bytes to 16 kilobytes. Despite this disadvantage, Flash is much more popular than EEPROM and is rapidly displacing many of the ROM devices as well.

The third member of the hybrid memory class is NVRAM (nonvolatile RAM). Non-volatility is also a characteristic of the ROM and hybrid memories discussed earlier. However, an NVRAM is physically very different from those devices. An NVRAM is usually just an SRAM with a battery backup. When the power is turned on, the NVRAM operates just like any other SRAM. But when the power is turned off, the NVRAM draws just enough electrical power from the battery to retain its current contents. NVRAM is fairly common in embedded systems. However, it is very expensive—even more expensive than SRAM—so its applications are typically limited to the storage of only a few hundred bytes of system-critical information that cannot be stored in any better way.

Table 6-1 summarizes the characteristics of different memory types.

Table 6-1. Memory Device Characteristics

Memory Type	Volatile?	Writeable?	Erase Size	Erase Cycles	Relative Cost	Relative Speed
SRAM	yes	yes	byte	unlimited	expensive	fast
DRAM	yes	yes	byte	unlimited	moderate	moderate
Masked ROM	no	no	n/a	n/a	inexpensive	fast
PROM	no	once, with programmer	n/a	n/a	moderate	fast
EPROM	no	yes, with programmer	entire chip	limited (see specs)	moderate	fast
EEPROM	no	yes	byte	limited (see specs)	expensive	fast to read, slow to write
Flash	no	yes	sector	limited (see specs)	moderate	fast to read, slow to write
NVRAM	no	yes	byte	none	expensive	fast

Memory Testing

One of the first pieces of serious embedded software you are likely to write is a memory test. Once the prototype hardware is ready, the designer would like some reassurance that she has wired the address and data lines correctly and that the memory chips are working properly. At first this might seem like a fairly simple assignment, but as you look at the problem more closely you will realize that it can be difficult to detect subtle memory problems with a simple test. In fact, as a result of programmer naiveté, many embedded systems include memory tests that would detect only the most catastrophic memory failures. Some of these might not even notice that the memory chips have been removed from the board!

Direct Memory Access

Direct memory access (DMA) is a technique for transferring blocks of data directly between two hardware devices. In the absence of DMA, the processor must read the data from one device and write it to the other, one byte or word at a time. If the amount of data to be transferred is large, or the frequency of transfers is high, the rest of the software might never get a chance to run. However, if a DMA controller is present it is possible to have it perform the entire transfer, with little assistance from the processor.

Here's how DMA works. When a block of data needs to be transferred, the processor provides the DMA controller with the source and destination addresses and the total number of bytes. The DMA controller then transfers the data from the source to the destination automatically. After each byte is copied, each address is incremented and the number of bytes remaining is reduced by one. When the number of bytes remaining reaches zero, the block transfer ends and the DMA controller sends an interrupt to the processor.

In a typical DMA scenario, the block of data is transferred directly to or from memory. For example, a network controller might want to place an incoming network packet into memory as it arrives, but only notify the processor once the entire packet has been received. By using DMA, the processor can spend more time processing the data once it arrives and less time transferring it between devices. The processor and DMA controller must share the address and data buses during this time, but this is handled automatically by the hardware and the processor is otherwise uninvolved with the actual transfer.

The purpose of a memory test is to confirm that each storage location in a memory device is working. In other words, if you store the number 50 at a particular address, you expect to find that number stored there until another number is written. The basic idea behind any memory test, then, is to write some set of data values to each address in the memory device and verify the data by reading it back. If all the values read back are the same as those that were written, then the memory device is said to pass the test. As you will see, it is only through careful selection of the set of data values that you can be sure that a passing result is meaningful.

Of course, a memory test like the one just described is unavoidably destructive. In the process of testing the memory, you must overwrite its prior contents. Because it is generally impractical to overwrite the contents of nonvolatile memories, the tests described in this section are generally used only for RAM testing. However, if the contents of a hybrid memory are unimportant—as they are during the product development stage—these same algorithms can be used to test those devices as well. The problem of validating the contents of a nonvolatile memory is addressed in a later section of this chapter.

Common Memory Problems

Before learning about specific test algorithms, you should be familiar with the types of memory problems that are likely to occur. One common misconception among software engineers is that most memory problems occur within the chips themselves. Though a major issue at one time (a few decades ago), problems of this type are increasingly rare. The manufacturers of memory devices perform a variety of post-production tests on each batch of chips. If there is a problem with a particular batch, it is extremely unlikely that one of the bad chips will make its way into your system.

The one type of memory chip problem you could encounter is a catastrophic failure. This is usually caused by some sort of physical or electrical damage received by the chip after manufacture. Catastrophic failures are uncommon and usually affect large portions of the chip. Because a large area is affected, it is reasonable to assume that catastrophic failure will be detected by any decent test algorithm.

In my experience, a more common source of memory problems is the circuit board. Typical circuit board problems are:

- Problems with the wiring between the processor and memory device

- Missing memory chips

- Improperly inserted memory chips

These are the problems that a good memory test algorithm should be able to detect. Such a test should also be able to detect catastrophic memory failures without specifically looking for them. So let's discuss circuit board problems in more detail.

Electrical wiring problems

An electrical wiring problem could be caused by an error in design or production of the board or as the result of damage received after manufacture. Each of the wires that connect the memory device to the processor is one of three types: an address line, a data line, or a control line. The address and data lines are used to select the memory location and to transfer the data, respectively. The control lines tell the memory device whether the processor wants to read or write the location and precisely when the data will be transferred. Unfortunately, one or more of these wires could be improperly routed or damaged in such a way that it is either shorted (i.e., connected to another wire on the board) or open (not connected to anything). These problems are often caused by a bit of solder splash or a broken trace, respectively. Both cases are illustrated in Figure 6-2.

Problems with the electrical connections to the processor will cause the memory device to behave incorrectly. Data might be stored incorrectly, stored at the wrong

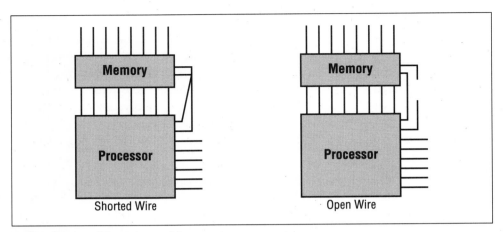

Figure 6-2. Possible wiring problems

address, or not stored at all. Each of these symptoms can be explained by wiring problems on the data, address, and control lines, respectively.

If the problem is with a data line, several data bits might appear to be "stuck together" (i.e., two or more bits always contain the same value, regardless of the data transmitted). Similarly, a data bit might be either "stuck high" (always 1) or "stuck low" (always 0). These problems can be detected by writing a sequence of data values designed to test that each data pin can be set to 0 and 1, independently of all the others.

If an address line has a wiring problem, the contents of two memory locations might appear to overlap. In other words, data written to one address will instead overwrite the contents of another address. This happens because an address bit that is shorted or open will cause the memory device to see an address different from the one selected by the processor.

Another possibility is that one of the control lines is shorted or open. Although it is theoretically possible to develop specific tests for control line problems, it is not possible to describe a general test for them. The operation of many control signals is specific to the processor or memory architecture. Fortunately, if there is a problem with a control line, the memory will probably not work at all, and this will be detected by other memory tests. If you suspect a problem with a control line, it is best to seek the advice of the board's designer before constructing a specific test.

Missing memory chips

A missing memory chip is clearly a problem that should be detected. Unfortunately, because of the capacitive nature of unconnected electrical wires, some memory tests will not detect this problem. For example, suppose you decided to use the following test algorithm: write the value 1 to the first location in memory, verify the value by reading it back, write 2 to the second location, verify the value, write 3 to the third location, verify, etc. Because each read occurs immediately after the corresponding write, it is possible that the data read back represents nothing more than the voltage remaining on the data bus from the previous write. If the data is read back too quickly, it will appear that the data has been correctly stored in memory—even though there is no memory chip at the other end of the bus!

To detect a missing memory chip, the test must be altered. Instead of performing the verification read immediately after the corresponding write, it is desirable to perform several consecutive writes followed by the same number of consecutive reads. For example, write the value 1 to the first location, 2 to the second location, and 3 to the third location, then verify the data at the first location, the second location, etc. If the data values are unique (as they are in the test just described), the missing chip will be detected: the first value read back will correspond to the last value written (3), rather than the first (1).

Improperly inserted chips

If a memory chip is present but improperly inserted in its socket, the system will usually behave as though there is a wiring problem or a missing chip. In other words, some number of the pins on the memory chip will either not be connected to the socket at all or will be connected at the wrong place. These pins will be part of the data bus, address bus, or control wiring. So as long as you test for wiring problems and missing chips, any improperly inserted chips will be detected automatically.

Before going on, let's quickly review the types of memory problems we must be able to detect. Memory chips only rarely have internal errors, but if they do, they are probably catastrophic in nature and will be detected by any test. A more common source of problems is the circuit board, where a wiring problem can occur or a memory chip might be missing or improperly inserted. Other memory problems can occur, but the ones described here are the most common and also the simplest to test in a generic way.

Developing a Test Strategy

By carefully selecting your test data and the order in which the addresses are tested, it is possible to detect all of the memory problems described earlier. It is usually best to break your memory test into small, single-minded pieces. This helps to improve the efficiency of the overall test and the readability of the code. More specific tests can also provide more detailed information about the source of the problem, if one is detected.

I have found it is best to have three individual memory tests: a data bus test, an address bus test, and a device test. The first two test for electrical wiring problems and improperly inserted chips; the third is intended to detect missing chips and catastrophic failures. As an unintended consequence, the device test will also uncover problems with the control bus wiring, though it cannot provide useful information about the source of such a problem.

The order in which you execute these three tests is important. The proper order is: data bus test first, followed by the address bus test, and then the device test. That's because the address bus test assumes a working data bus, and the device test results are meaningless unless both the address and data buses are known to be good. If any of the tests fail, you should work with a hardware engineer to locate the source of the problem. By looking at the data value or address at which the test failed, she should be able to quickly isolate the problem on the circuit board.

Data bus test

The first thing we want to test is the data bus wiring. We need to confirm that any value placed on the data bus by the processor is correctly received by the memory device at the other end. The most obvious way to test that is to write all possible data values and verify that the memory device stores each one successfully. However, that is not the most efficient test available. A faster method is to test the bus one bit at a time. The data bus passes the test if each data bit can be set to 0 and 1, independently of the other data bits.

A good way to test each bit independently is to perform the so-called "walking 1's test." Table 6-2 shows the data patterns used in an 8-bit version of this test. The name, walking 1's, comes from the fact that a single data bit is set to 1 and "walked" through the entire data word. The number of data values to test is the same as the width of the data bus. This reduces the number of test patterns from 2^n to n, where n is the width of the data bus.

Table 6-2. Consecutive Data Values for the Walking 1's Test

00000001
00000010
00000100
00001000
00010000
00100000
01000000
10000000

Because we are testing only the data bus at this point, all of the data values can be written to the same address. Any address within the memory device will do. However, if the data bus splits as it makes its way to more than one memory chip, you will need to perform the data bus test at multiple addresses, one within each chip.

To perform the walking 1's test, simply write the first data value in the table, verify it by reading it back, write the second value, verify, etc. When you reach the end of the table, the test is complete. It is okay to do the read immediately after the corresponding write this time because we are not yet looking for missing chips. In fact, this test may provide meaningful results even if the memory chips are not installed!

The function *memTestDataBus* shows how to implement the walking 1's test in C. It assumes that the caller will select the test address, and tests the entire set of data values at that address. If the data bus is working properly, the function will return 0. Otherwise it will return the data value for which the test failed. The bit that is set in the returned value corresponds to the first faulty data line, if any.

```c
typedef unsigned char datum;       /* Set the data bus width to 8 bits. */

/**********************************************************************
 *
 * Function:    memTestDataBus()
 *
 * Description: Test the data bus wiring in a memory region by
 *              performing a walking 1's test at a fixed address
 *              within that region.  The address (and hence the
 *              memory region) is selected by the caller.
 *
 * Notes:
 *
 * Returns:     0 if the test succeeds.
 *              A nonzero result is the first pattern that failed.
 *
 **********************************************************************/
datum
memTestDataBus(volatile datum * address)
{
    datum pattern;


    /*
     * Perform a walking 1's test at the given address.
     */
    for (pattern = 1; pattern != 0; pattern <<= 1)
    {
        /*
         * Write the test pattern.
         */
        *address = pattern;
```

```
          /*
           * Read it back (immediately is okay for this test).
           */
          if (*address != pattern)
          {
              return (pattern);
          }
      }

      return (0);

  }   /* memTestDataBus() */
```

Address bus test

After confirming that the data bus works properly, you should next test the address bus. Remember that address bus problems lead to overlapping memory locations. There are many possible addresses that could overlap. However, it is not necessary to check every possible combination. You should instead follow the example of the previous data bus test and try to isolate each address bit during testing. You simply need to confirm that each of the address pins can be set to 0 and 1 without affecting any of the others.

The smallest set of addresses that will cover all possible combinations is the set of "power-of-two" addresses. These addresses are analogous to the set of data values used in the walking 1's test. The corresponding memory locations are 00001h, 00002h, 00004h, 00008h, 00010h, 00020h, and so forth. In addition, address 00000h must also be tested. The possibility of overlapping locations makes the address bus test harder to implement. After writing to one of the addresses, you must check that none of the others has been overwritten.

It is important to note that not all of the address lines can be tested in this way. Part of the address—the leftmost bits—selects the memory chip itself. Another part—the rightmost bits—might not be significant if the data bus width is greater than 8 bits. These extra bits will remain constant throughout the test and reduce the number of test addresses. For example, if the processor has 20 address bits, as the 80188EB does, then it can address up to 1 megabyte of memory. If you want to test a 128-kilobyte block of memory, the three most significant address bits will remain constant.* In that case, only the 17 rightmost bits of the address bus can actually be tested.

To confirm that no two memory locations overlap, you should first write some initial data value at each power-of-two offset within the device. Then write a new value—an inverted copy of the initial value is a good choice—to the first test

---

* 128 kilobytes is one-eighth of the total 1-megabyte address space.

offset, and verify that the initial data value is still stored at every other power-of-two offset. If you find a location (other than the one just written) that contains the new data value, you have found a problem with the current address bit. If no overlapping is found, repeat the procedure for each of the remaining offsets.

The function *memTestAddressBus* shows how this can be done in practice. The function accepts two parameters. The first parameter is the base address of the memory block to be tested, and the second is its size, in bytes. The size is used to determine which address bits should be tested. For best results, the base address should contain a 0 in each of those bits. If the address bus test fails, the address at which the first error was detected will be returned. Otherwise, this function returns NULL to indicate success.

```
/*********************************************************************
 *
 * Function:     memTestAddressBus()
 *
 * Description:  Test the address bus wiring in a memory region by
 *               performing a walking 1's test on the relevant bits
 *               of the address and checking for aliasing.  The test
 *               will find single-bit address failures such as stuck
 *               -high, stuck-low, and shorted pins.  The base address
 *               and size of the region are selected by the caller.
 *
 * Notes:        For best results, the selected base address should
 *               have enough LSB 0's to guarantee single address bit
 *               changes.  For example, to test a 64 KB region, select
 *               a base address on a 64 KB boundary.  Also, select the
 *               region size as a power-of-two--if at all possible.
 *
 * Returns:      NULL if the test succeeds.
 *               A nonzero result is the first address at which an
 *               aliasing problem was uncovered.  By examining the
 *               contents of memory, it may be possible to gather
 *               additional information about the problem.
 *
 *********************************************************************/
datum *
memTestAddressBus(volatile datum * baseAddress, unsigned long nBytes)
{
    unsigned long addressMask = (nBytes - 1) >> 2;
    unsigned long offset;
    unsigned long testOffset;

    datum pattern     = 0xAA;
    datum antipattern = 0x55;

    /*
     * Write the default pattern at each of the power-of-two offsets.
     */
    for (offset = sizeof(datum); (offset & addressMask) != 0; offset <<= 1)
    {
```

```
        baseAddress[offset] = pattern;
    }

    /*
     * Check for address bits stuck high.
     */
    testOffset = 0;
    baseAddress[testOffset] = antipattern;

    for (offset = sizeof(datum); (offset & addressMask) != 0; offset <<= 1)
    {
        if (baseAddress[offset] != pattern)
        {
            return ((datum *) &baseAddress[offset]);
        }
    }

    baseAddress[testOffset] = pattern;

    /*
     * Check for address bits stuck low or shorted.
     */
    for (testOffset = sizeof(datum); (testOffset & addressMask) != 0;
            testOffset <<= 1)
    {
        baseAddress[testOffset] = antipattern;

        for (offset = sizeof(datum); (offset & addressMask) != 0;
                offset <<= 1)
        {
            if ((baseAddress[offset] != pattern) && (offset != testOffset))
            {
                return ((datum *) &baseAddress[testOffset]);
            }
        }

        baseAddress[testOffset] = pattern;
    }

    return (NULL);

}   /* memTestAddressBus() */
```

Device test

Once you know that the address and data bus wiring are correct, it is necessary to test the integrity of the memory device itself. The thing to test is that every bit in the device is capable of holding both 0 and 1. This is a fairly straightforward test to implement, but it takes significantly longer to execute than the previous two.

For a complete device test, you must visit (write and verify) every memory location twice. You are free to choose any data value for the first pass, so long as you invert that value during the second. And because there is a possibility of missing memory chips, it is best to select a set of data that changes with (but is not equivalent to) the address. A simple example is an increment test.

The data values for the increment test are shown in the first two columns of Table 6-3. The third column shows the inverted data values used during the second pass of this test. The second pass represents a decrement test. There are many other possible choices of data, but the incrementing data pattern is adequate and easy to compute.

Table 6-3. Data Values for an Increment Test

Memory Offset	Binary Value	Inverted Value
000h	00000001	11111110
001h	00000010	11111101
002h	00000011	11111100
003h	00000100	11111011
...	...	...
0FEh	11111111	00000000
0FFh	00000000	11111111

The function *memTestDevice* implements just such a two-pass increment/decrement test. It accepts two parameters from the caller. The first parameter is the starting address, and the second is the number of bytes to be tested. These parameters give the user a maximum of control over which areas of memory will be overwritten. The function will return **NULL** on success. Otherwise, the first address that contains an incorrect data value is returned.

```
/**********************************************************************
 *
 * Function:    memTestDevice()
 *
 * Description: Test the integrity of a physical memory device by
 *              performing an increment/decrement test over the
 *              entire region.  In the process every storage bit
 *              in the device is tested as a zero and a one.  The
 *              base address and the size of the region are
 *              selected by the caller.
 *
 * Notes:
 *
 * Returns:     NULL if the test succeeds.  Also, in that case, the
 *              entire memory region will be filled with zeros.
 *
 *              A nonzero result is the first address at which an
 *              incorrect value was read back.  By examining the
 *              contents of memory, it may be possible to gather
 *              additional information about the problem.
 *
 **********************************************************************/
```

```
datum *
memTestDevice(volatile datum * baseAddress, unsigned long nBytes)
{
    unsigned long offset;
    unsigned long nWords = nBytes / sizeof(datum);

    datum pattern;
    datum antipattern;

    /*
     * Fill memory with a known pattern.
     */
    for (pattern = 1, offset = 0; offset < nWords; pattern++, offset++)
    {
        baseAddress[offset] = pattern;
    }

    /*
     * Check each location and invert it for the second pass.
     */
    for (pattern = 1, offset = 0; offset < nWords; pattern++, offset++)
    {
        if (baseAddress[offset] != pattern)
        {
            return ((datum *) &baseAddress[offset]);
        }

        antipattern = ~pattern;
        baseAddress[offset] = antipattern;
    }

    /*
     * Check each location for the inverted pattern and zero it.
     */
    for (pattern = 1, offset = 0; offset < nWords; pattern++, offset++)
    {
        antipattern = ~pattern;
        if (baseAddress[offset] != antipattern)
        {
            return ((datum *) &baseAddress[offset]);
        }

        baseAddress[offset] = 0;
    }

    return (NULL);

}   /* memTestDevice() */
```

Putting it all together

To make our discussion more concrete, let's consider a practical example. Suppose that we wanted to test the second 64-kilobyte chunk of the SRAM on the Arcom board. To do this, we would call each of the three test routines in turn. In each case, the first parameter would be the base address of the memory block.

Looking at our memory map, we see that the physical address is 10000h, which is represented by the segment:offset pair `0x1000:0000`. The width of the data bus is 8 bits (a feature of the 80188EB processor), and there are a total of 64 kilobytes to be tested (corresponding to the rightmost 16 bits of the address bus).

If any of the memory test routines returns a nonzero (or non-NULL) value, we'll immediately turn on the red LED to visually indicate the error. Otherwise, after all three tests have completed successfully, we will turn on the green LED. In the event of an error, the test routine that failed will return some information about the problem encountered. This information can be useful when communicating with a hardware engineer about the nature of the problem. However, it is visible only if we are running the test program in a debugger or emulator.

The best way to proceed is to assume the best, download the test program, and let it run to completion. Then, if and only if the red LED comes on, must you use the debugger to step through the program and examine the return codes and contents of the memory to see which test failed and why.

```c
#include "led.h"

#define BASE_ADDRESS    (volatile datum *) 0x10000000
#define NUM_BYTES       0x10000


/**********************************************************************
 *
 * Function:    main()
 *
 * Description: Test the second 64 KB bank of SRAM.
 *
 * Notes:
 *
 * Returns:     0 on success.
 *              Otherwise -1 indicates failure.
 *
 **********************************************************************/
main(void)
{
    if ((memTestDataBus(BASE_ADDRESS) != 0) ||
        (memTestAddressBus(BASE_ADDRESS, NUM_BYTES) != NULL) ||
        (memTestDevice(BASE_ADDRESS, NUM_BYTES) != NULL))
    {
        toggleLed(LED_RED);
        return (-1);
    }
    else
    {
        toggleLed(LED_GREEN);
        return (0);
    }

}   /* main() */
```

Unfortunately, it is not always possible to write memory tests in a high-level language. For example, C and C++ both require the use of a stack. But a stack itself requires working memory. This might be reasonable in a system that has more than one memory device. For example, you might create a stack in an area of RAM that is already known to be working, while testing another memory device. In a common such situation, a small SRAM could be tested from assembly and the stack could be created there afterward. Then a larger block of DRAM could be tested using a nicer test algorithm, like the one shown earlier. If you cannot assume enough working RAM for the stack and data needs of the test program, then you will need to rewrite these memory test routines entirely in assembly language.

Another option is to run the memory test program from an emulator. In this case, you could choose to place the stack in an area of the emulator's own internal memory. By moving the emulator's internal memory around in the target memory map, you could systematically test each memory device on the target.

The need for memory testing is perhaps most apparent during product development, when the reliability of the hardware and its design are still unproved. However, memory is one of the most critical resources in any embedded system, so it might also be desirable to include a memory test in the final release of your software. In that case, the memory test and other hardware confidence tests should be run each time the system is powered-on or reset. Together, this initial test suite forms a set of hardware diagnostics. If one or more of the diagnostics fail, a repair technician can be called in to diagnose the problem and repair or replace the faulty hardware.

Validating Memory Contents

It does not usually make sense to perform the type of memory testing described earlier when dealing with ROM and hybrid memory devices. ROM devices cannot be written at all, and hybrid devices usually contain data or programs that cannot be overwritten. However, it should be clear that the same sorts of memory problems can occur with these devices. A chip might be missing or improperly inserted or physically or electrically damaged, or there could be an electrical wiring problem. Rather than just assuming that these nonvolatile memory devices are functioning properly, you would be better off having some way to confirm that the device is working and that the data it contains is valid. That's where checksums and cyclic redundancy codes come in.

Checksums

How can we tell if the data or program stored in a nonvolatile memory device is still valid? One of the easiest ways is to compute a checksum of the data when it is known to be good—prior to programming the ROM, for example. Then, each time you want to confirm the validity of the data, you need only recalculate the checksum and compare the result to the previously computed value. If the two checksums match, the data is assumed to be valid. By carefully selecting the checksum algorithm, we can increase the probability that specific types of errors will be detected.

The simplest checksum algorithm is to add up all the data bytes (or, if you prefer a 16-bit checksum, words), discarding carries along the way. A noteworthy weakness of this algorithm is that if all of the data (including the stored checksum) is accidentally overwritten with 0's, then this data corruption will be undetectable. The sum of a large block of zeros is also zero. The simplest way to overcome this weakness is to add a final step to the checksum algorithm: invert the result. That way, if the data and checksum are somehow overwritten with 0's, the test will fail because the proper checksum would be FFh.

Unfortunately, a simple sum-of-data checksum like this one cannot detect many of the most common data errors. Clearly if one bit of data is corrupted (switched from 1 to 0, or vice versa), the error would be detected. But what if two bits from the very same "column" happened to be corrupted alternately (the first switches from 1 to 0, the other from 0 to 1)? The proper checksum does not change, and the error would not be detected. If bit errors can occur, you will probably want to use a better checksum algorithm. We'll see one of these in the next section.

After computing the expected checksum, we'll need a place to store it. One option is to compute the checksum ahead of time and define it as a constant in the routine that verifies the data. This method is attractive to the programmer but has several shortcomings. Foremost among them is the possibility that the data—and, as a result, the expected checksum—might change during the lifetime of the product. This is particularly likely if the data being tested is actually embedded software that will be periodically updated as bugs are fixed or new features added.

A better idea is to store the checksum at some fixed location in memory. For example, you might decide to use the very last location of the memory device being verified. This makes insertion of the checksum easy—just compute the checksum and insert it into the memory image prior to programming the memory device. When you recalculate the checksum, you simply skip over the location that contains the expected result, and compare the new result to the value stored there. Another good place to store the checksum is in another nonvolatile memory device. Both of these solutions work very well in practice.

Cyclic Redundancy Codes

A cyclic redundancy code (CRC) is a specific checksum algorithm that is designed to detect the most common data errors. The theory behind the CRC is quite mathematical and beyond the scope of this book. However, cyclic redundancy codes are frequently useful in embedded applications that require the storage or transmission of large blocks of data. What follows is a brief explanation of the CRC technique and some source code that shows how it can be done in C. Thankfully, you don't need to understand why CRCs detect data errors—or even how they are implemented—to take advantage of their ability to detect errors.

Here's a very brief explanation of the mathematics. When computing a CRC, you consider the set of data to be a very long string of 1's and 0's (called the *message*). This binary string is divided—in a rather peculiar way—by a smaller fixed binary string called the *generator polynomial*. The *remainder* of this binary long division is the CRC checksum. By carefully selecting the generator polynomial for certain desirable mathematical properties, you can use the resulting checksum to detect most (but never all) errors within the message. The strongest of these generator polynomials are able to detect all single and double bit errors, and all odd-length strings of consecutive error bits. In addition, greater than 99.99% of all burst errors—defined as a sequence of bits that has one error at each end—can be detected. Together, these types of errors account for a large percentage of the possible errors within any stored or transmitted binary message.

Those generator polynomials with the very best error-detection capabilities are frequently adopted as international standards. Three such standards are parameterized in Table 6-4. Associated with each standard are its width (in bits), the generator polynomial, a binary representation of the polynomial called the divisor, an initial value for the remainder, and a value to XOR (exclusive or) with the final remainder.[*]

Table 6-4. International Standard Generator Polynomials

	CCITT	CRC16	CRC32
Checksum size (width)	16 bits	16 bits	32 bits
Generator polynomial	$x^{16} + x^{12} + x^5 + 1$	$x^{16} + x^{15} + x^2 + 1$	$x^{32} + x^{26} + x^{23} + x^{22} + x^{16} + x^{12} + x^{11} + x^{10} + x^8 + x^7 + x^5 + x^4 + x^2 + x^1 + 1$
Divisor (polynomial)	0x1021	0x8005	0x04C11DB7
Initial remainder	0xFFFF	0x0000	0xFFFFFFFF
Final XOR value	0x0000	0x0000	0xFFFFFFFF

---

[*] The divisor is simply a binary representation of the coefficients of the generator polynomial—each of which is either 0 or 1. To make this even more confusing, the highest-order coefficient of the generator polynomial (always a 1) is left out of the binary representation. For example, the polynomial in the first standard, CCITT, has four nonzero coefficients. But the corresponding binary representation has only three 1's in it (bits 12, 5, and 0).

The code that follows can be used to compute any CRC formula that has a similar set of parameters.* To make this as easy as possible, I have defined all of the CRC parameters as constants. To change to the CRC16 standard, simply change the values of the three constants. For CRC32, change the three constants and redefine `width` as type `unsigned long`.

```
/*
 * The CRC parameters.  Currently configured for CCITT.
 * Simply modify these to switch to another CRC standard.
 */
#define POLYNOMIAL          0x1021
#define INITIAL_REMAINDER   0xFFFF
#define FINAL_XOR_VALUE     0x0000


/*
 * The width of the CRC calculation and result.
 * Modify the typedef for an 8 or 32-bit CRC standard.
 */
typedef unsigned short width;

#define WIDTH   (8 * sizeof(width))
#define TOPBIT  (1 << (WIDTH - 1))
```

The function *crcInit* should be called first. It implements the peculiar binary division required by the CRC algorithm. It will precompute the remainder for each of the 256 possible values of a byte of the message data. These intermediate results are stored in a global lookup table that can be used by the *crcCompute* function. By doing it this way, the CRC of a large message can be computed a byte at a time rather than bit by bit. This reduces the CRC calculation time significantly.

```
/*
 * An array containing the pre-computed intermediate result for each
 * possible byte of input.  This is used to speed up the computation.
 */
width  crcTable[256];

/**********************************************************************
 *
 * Function:    crcInit()
 *
 * Description: Initialize the CRC lookup table.  This table is used
 *              by crcCompute() to make CRC computation faster.
 *
 * Notes:       The mod-2 binary long division is implemented here.
 *
 * Returns:     None defined.
 *
 **********************************************************************/
```

---

* There is one other potential twist called "reflection" that my code does not support. You probably won't need that anyway.

```
void
crcInit(void)
{
    width  remainder;
    width  dividend;
    int    bit;


    /*
     * Perform binary long division, a bit at a time.
     */
    for (dividend = 0; dividend < 256; dividend++)
    {
        /*
         * Initialize the remainder.
         */
        remainder = dividend << (WIDTH - 8);

        /*
         * Shift and XOR with the polynomial.
         */
        for (bit = 0; bit < 8; bit++)
        {
            /*
             * Try to divide the current data bit.
             */
            if (remainder & TOPBIT)
            {
                remainder = (remainder << 1) ^ POLYNOMIAL;
            }
            else
            {
                remainder = remainder << 1;
            }
        }

        /*
         * Save the result in the table.
         */
        crcTable[dividend] = remainder;
    }

}   /* crcInit() */
```

Finally, we arrive at the actual workhorse routine, *crcCompute*. This is a routine that you can call over and over from your application to compute and verify CRC checksums. An additional benefit of splitting the computation between *crcInit* and *crcCompute* is that the *crcInit* function need not be executed on the embedded system. Instead, this function can be run in advance—on any computer—to produce the contents of the lookup table. The values in the table can then be stored in ROM (requiring only 256 bytes of storage) and referenced over and over by *crcCompute*.

```
/*********************************************************************
 *
 * Function:     crcCompute()
 *
 * Description: Compute the CRC checksum of a binary message block.
 *
 * Notes:        This function expects that crcInit() has been called
 *               first to initialize the CRC lookup table.
 *
 * Returns:      The CRC of the data.
 *
 *********************************************************************/
width
crcCompute(unsigned char * message, unsigned int nBytes)
{
    unsigned int    offset;
    unsigned char   byte;
    width           remainder = INITIAL_REMAINDER;


    /*
     * Divide the message by the polynomial, a byte at a time.
     */
    for (offset = 0; offset < nBytes; offset++)
    {
        byte = (remainder >> (WIDTH - 8)) ^ message[offset];
        remainder = crcTable[byte] ^ (remainder << 8);
    }

    /*
     * The final remainder is the CRC result.
     */
    return (remainder ^ FINAL_XOR_VALUE);

}   /* crcCompute() */
```

Working with Flash Memory

From the programmer's viewpoint, Flash is arguably the most complicated memory device ever invented. The hardware interface has improved somewhat since the original devices were introduced in 1988, but there is still a long way to go. Reading from Flash memory is fast and easy, as it should be. In fact, reading data from a Flash is not all that different from reading from any other memory device.[*] The processor simply provides the address, and the memory device returns the data stored at that location. Most Flash devices enter this type of "read" mode

---

[*] There is one small difference worth noting here. The erase and write cycles take longer than the read cycle. So if a read is attempted in the middle of one of those operations, the result will be either delayed or incorrect, depending on the device.

automatically whenever the system is reset; no special initialization sequence is required to enable reading.

Writing data to a Flash is much harder. Three factors make writes difficult. First, each memory location must be erased before it can be rewritten. If the old data is not erased, the result of the write operation will be some logical combination of the old and new values, and the stored value will usually be something other than what you intended.

The second thing that makes writes to a Flash difficult is that only one sector, or block, of the device can be erased at a time; it is impossible to erase a single byte. The size of an individual sector varies by device, but it is usually on the order of several thousand bytes. For example, the Flash device on the Arcom board—an AMD 29F010—has eight sectors, each containing 16 kilobytes.

Finally, the process of erasing the old data and writing the new varies from one manufacturer to another and is usually rather complicated. These device programming interfaces are so awkward that it is usually best to add a layer of software to make the Flash memory easier to use. If implemented, this hardware-specific layer of software is usually called the Flash driver.

Flash Drivers

Because it can be difficult to write data to the Flash device, it often makes sense to create a Flash driver. The purpose of the Flash driver is to hide the details of a specific chip from the rest of the software. This driver should present a simple application programming interface (API) consisting of the erase and write operations. Parts of the application software that need to modify data stored in Flash memory simply call the driver to handle the details. This allows the application programmer to make high-level requests like "erase the block at address D0000h" or "write a block of data, beginning at address D4000h." It also keeps the device-specific code separate, so it can be easily modified if another manufacturer's Flash device is later used.

A Flash driver for the AMD 29F010 device on the Arcom board is shown below. This driver contains just two functions: *flashErase* and *flashWrite*. These functions erase an entire sector and write an array of bytes, respectively. You should be able to see from the code listings that the interaction with the Flash device is no picnic. This code will work only with an AMD 29F010 device. However, the same API could be used with any Flash memory device.

```
#include "tgt188eb.h"

/*
 * Features of the AMD 29F010 Flash memory device.
 */
```

```
#define FLASH_SIZE              0x20000
#define FLASH_BLOCK_SIZE        0x04000

#define UNLOCK1_OFFSET          0x5555
#define UNLOCK2_OFFSET          0x2AAA
#define COMMAND_OFFSET          0x5555

#define FLASH_CMD_UNLOCK1       0xAA
#define FLASH_CMD_UNLOCK2       0x55
#define FLASH_CMD_READ_RESET    0xF0
#define FLASH_CMD_AUTOSELECT    0x90
#define FLASH_CMD_BYTE_PROGRAM  0xA0
#define FLASH_CMD_ERASE_SETUP   0x80
#define FLASH_CMD_CHIP_ERASE    0x10
#define FLASH_CMD_SECTOR_ERASE  0x30

#define DQ7     0x80
#define DQ5     0x20


/**********************************************************************
 *
 * Function:    flashWrite()
 *
 * Description: Write data to consecutive locations in the Flash.
 *
 * Notes:       This function is specific to the AMD 29F010 Flash
 *              memory.  In that device, a byte that has been
 *              previously written must be erased before it can be
 *              rewritten successfully.
 *
 * Returns:     The number of bytes successfully written.
 *
 **********************************************************************/
int
flashWrite(unsigned char *       baseAddress,
           const unsigned char   data[],
           unsigned int          nBytes)
{
    unsigned char * flashBase = FLASH_BASE;
    unsigned int    offset;

    for (offset = 0; offset < nBytes; offset++)
    {
        /*
         * Issue the command sequence for byte program.
         */
        flashBase[UNLOCK1_OFFSET] = FLASH_CMD_UNLOCK1;
        flashBase[UNLOCK2_OFFSET] = FLASH_CMD_UNLOCK2;
        flashBase[COMMAND_OFFSET] = FLASH_CMD_BYTE_PROGRAM;

        /*
         * Perform the actual write operation.
         */
        baseAddress[offset] = data[offset];
```

```
        /*
         * Wait for the operation to complete or time-out.
         */
        while (((baseAddress[offset] & DQ7) != (data[offset] & DQ7)) &&
                !(baseAddress[offset] & DQ5));

        if ((baseAddress[offset] & DQ7) != (data[offset] & DQ7))
        {
            break;
        }
    }

    return (offset);

}   /* flashWrite() */

/**********************************************************************
 *
 * Function:     flashErase()
 *
 * Description: Erase a block of the Flash memory device.
 *
 * Notes:        This function is specific to the AMD 29F010 Flash
 *               memory.  In this device, individual sectors may be
 *               hardware protected.  If this algorithm encounters
 *               a protected sector, the erase operation will fail
 *               without notice.
 *
 * Returns:      O on success.
 *               Otherwise -1 indicates failure.
 *
 **********************************************************************/
int
flashErase(unsigned char * sectorAddress)
{
    unsigned char * flashBase = FLASH_BASE;

    /*
     * Issue the command sequence for sector erase.
     */
    flashBase[UNLOCK1_OFFSET] = FLASH_CMD_UNLOCK1;
    flashBase[UNLOCK2_OFFSET] = FLASH_CMD_UNLOCK2;
    flashBase[COMMAND_OFFSET] = FLASH_CMD_ERASE_SETUP;
    flashBase[UNLOCK1_OFFSET] = FLASH_CMD_UNLOCK1;
    flashBase[UNLOCK2_OFFSET] = FLASH_CMD_UNLOCK2;

    *sectorAddress = FLASH_CMD_SECTOR_ERASE;

    /*
     * Wait for the operation to complete or time-out.
     */
    while (!(*sectorAddress & DQ7) && !(*sectorAddress & DQ5));
```

```
        if (!(*sectorAddress & DQ7))
        {
            return (-1);
        }

        return (0);

    }   /* flashErase() */
```

Of course, this is just one possible way to interface to a Flash memory—and not a particularly advanced one at that. In particular, this implementation does not handle any of the chip's possible errors. What if the erase operation never completes? The function *flashErase* will just keep spinning its wheels, waiting for that to occur. A more robust implementation would use a software time-out as a backup. For example, if the Flash device doesn't respond within twice the maximum expected time (as stated in the databook), the routine could stop polling and indicate the error to the caller (or user) in some way.

Another thing that people sometimes do with Flash memory is to implement a small filesystem. Because the Flash memory provides nonvolatile storage that is also rewriteable, it can be thought of as similar to any other secondary storage system, such as a hard drive. In the filesystem case, the functions provided by the driver would be more file-oriented. Standard filesystem functions like *open, close, read,* and *write* provide a good starting point for the driver's programming interface. The underlying filesystem structure can be as simple or complex as your system requires. However, a well-understood format like the File Allocation Table (FAT) structure used by DOS is good enough for most embedded projects.

7

Peripherals

In this chapter:
- *Control and Status Registers*
- *The Device Driver Philosophy*
- *A Simple Timer Driver*
- *Das Blinkenlights, Revisited*

> *Each pizza glides into a slot like a circuit board into a computer, clicks into place as the smart box interfaces with the onboard system of the car. The address of the customer is communicated to the car, which computes and projects the optimal route on a heads-up display.*
>
> —Neal Stephenson
> *Snow Crash*

In addition to the processor and memory, most embedded systems contain a handful of other hardware devices. Some of these devices are specific to the application domain, while others—like timers and serial ports—are useful in a wide variety of systems. The most generically useful of these are often included within the same chip as the processor and are called internal, or on-chip, peripherals. Hardware devices that reside outside the processor chip are, therefore, said to be external peripherals. In this chapter we'll discuss the most common software issues that arise when interfacing to a peripheral of either type.

Control and Status Registers

The basic interface between an embedded processor and a peripheral device is a set of control and status registers. These registers are part of the peripheral hardware, and their locations, size, and individual meanings are features of the peripheral. For example, the registers within a serial controller are very different from those in a timer/counter. In this section, I'll describe how to manipulate the contents of these control and status registers directly from your C/C++ programs.

Depending upon the design of the processor and board, peripheral devices are located either in the processor's memory space or within the I/O space. In fact, it is common for embedded systems to include some peripherals of each type. These are called memory-mapped and I/O-mapped peripherals, respectively. Of the two types, memory-mapped peripherals are generally easier to work with and are increasingly popular.

Memory-mapped control and status registers can be made to look just like ordinary variables. To do this, you need simply declare a pointer to the register, or block of registers, and set the value of the pointer explicitly. For example, if the P2LTCH register from Chapter 2, *Your First Embedded Program*, were memory-mapped and located at physical address 7205Eh, we could have implemented *toggleLed* entirely in C, as shown below. A pointer to an **unsigned short**—a 16-bit register—is declared and explicitly initialized to the address 0x7200:005E. From that point on, the pointer to the register looks just like a pointer to any other integer variable:

```
unsigned short * pP2LTCH = (unsigned short *) 0x7200005E;

void
toggleLed(void)
{
    *pP2LTCH ^= LED_GREEN;                /* Read, xor, and modify.    */

}   /* toggleLed() */
```

Note, however, that there is one very important difference between device registers and ordinary variables. The contents of a device register can change without the knowledge or intervention of your program. That's because the register contents can also be modified by the peripheral hardware. By contrast, the contents of a variable will not change unless your program modifies them explicitly. For that reason, we say that the contents of a device register are volatile, or subject to change without notice.

The C/C++ keyword **volatile** should be used when declaring pointers to device registers. This warns the compiler not to make any assumptions about the data stored at that address. For example, if the compiler sees a write to the volatile location followed by another write to that same location, it will not assume that the first write is an unnecessary use of processor time. In other words, the keyword **volatile** instructs the optimization phase of the compiler to treat that variable as though its behavior cannot be predicted at compile time.

Here's an example of the use of **volatile** to warn the compiler about the P2LTCH register in the previous code listing:

```
volatile unsigned short * pP2LTCH = (unsigned short *) 0x7200005E;
```

It would be wrong to interpret this statement to mean that the pointer itself is volatile. In fact, the value of the variable **pP2LTCH** will remain 0x7200005E for the duration of the program (unless it is changed somewhere else, of course). Rather, it is the data pointed to that is subject to change without notice. This is a very subtle point, and it is easy to confuse yourself by thinking about it too much. Just remember that the location of a register is fixed, though its contents might not be. And if you use the `volatile` keyword, the compiler will assume the same.

The primary disadvantage of the other type of device registers, I/O-mapped registers, is that there is no standard way to access them from C or C++. Such registers are accessible only with the help of special machine-language instructions. And these processor-specific instructions are not supported by the C or C++ language standards. So it is necessary to use special library routines or inline assembly (as we did in Chapter 2) to read and write the registers of an I/O–mapped device.

The Device Driver Philosophy

When it comes to designing device drivers, you should always focus on one easily stated goal: hide the hardware completely. When you're finished, you want the device driver module to be the only piece of software in the entire system that reads or writes that particular device's control and status registers directly. In addition, if the device generates any interrupts, the interrupt service routine that responds to them should be an integral part of the device driver. In this section, I'll explain why I recommend this philosophy and how it can be achieved.

Of course, attempts to hide the hardware completely are difficult. Any programming interface you select will reflect the broad features of the device. That's to be expected. The goal should be to create a programming interface that would not need to be changed if the underlying peripheral were replaced with another in its general class. For example, all Flash memory devices share the concepts of sectors (though the sector size can differ between chips). An erase operation can be performed only on an entire sector, and once erased, individual bytes or words can be rewritten. So the programming interface provided by the Flash driver example in the last chapter should work with any Flash memory device. The specific features of the AMD 29F010 are hidden from that level, as desired.

Device drivers for embedded systems are quite different from their workstation counterparts. In a modern computer workstation, device drivers are most often concerned with satisfying the requirements of the operating system. For example, workstation operating systems generally impose strict requirements on the software interface between themselves and a network card. The device driver for a particular network card must conform to this software interface, regardless of the features and capabilities of the underlying hardware. Application programs that want to use the network card are forced to use the networking API provided by the operating system and don't have direct access to the card itself. In this case, the goal of hiding the hardware completely is easily met.

By contrast, the application software in an embedded system can easily access your hardware. In fact, because all of the software is linked together into a single binary image, there is rarely even a distinction made between application software, operating system, and device drivers. The drawing of these lines and the enforcement of hardware access restrictions are purely the responsibilities of the software developers. Both are design decisions that the developers must consciously make. In other words, the implementers of embedded software can more easily cheat on the software design than their non-embedded peers.

The benefits of good device driver design are threefold. First, because of the modularization, the structure of the overall software is easier to understand. Second, because there is only one module that ever interacts directly with the peripheral's registers, the state of the hardware can be more accurately tracked. And, last but not least, software changes that result from hardware changes are localized to the device driver. Each of these benefits can and will help to reduce the total number of bugs in your embedded software. But you have to be willing to put in a bit of extra effort at design time in order to realize such savings.

If you agree with the philosophy of hiding all hardware specifics and interactions within the device driver, it will usually consist of the five components in the following list. To make driver implementation as simple and incremental as possible, these elements should be developed in the order in which they are presented.

1. A data structure that overlays the memory-mapped control and status registers of the device

The first step in the driver development process is to create a C-style `struct` that looks just like the memory-mapped registers of your device. This usually involves studying the data book for the peripheral and creating a table of the control and status registers and their offsets. Then, beginning with the register at the lowest offset, start filling out the `struct`. (If one or more locations are unused or reserved, be sure to place dummy variables there to fill in the additional space.)

An example of such a data structure is shown below. This structure describes the registers in one of the on-chip timer/counter units within the 80188EB processor. The device has three registers, arranged as shown in the `TimerCounter` data structure below. Each register is 16 bits wide and should be treated as an unsigned integer, although one of them, the `control` register, is actually a collection of individually significant bits.

```
struct TimerCounter
{
    unsigned short  count;          // Current Count, offset 0x00
    unsigned short  maxCountA;      // Maximum Count, offset 0x02
    unsigned short  _reserved;      // Unused Space,  offset 0x04
    unsigned short  control;        // Control Bits,  offset 0x06
};
```

To make the bits within the control register easier to read and write individually, we might also define the following bitmasks:

```
#define TIMER_ENABLE    0xC000      // Enable the timer.
#define TIMER_DISABLE   0x4000      // Disable the timer.
#define TIMER_INTERRUPT 0x2000      // Enable timer interrupts.
#define TIMER_MAXCOUNT  0x0020      // Timer complete?
#define TIMER_PERIODIC  0x0001      // Periodic timer?
```

2. A set of variables to track the current state of the hardware and device driver

The second step in the driver development process is to figure out what variables you will need to track the state of the hardware and device driver. For example, in the case of the timer/counter unit described earlier we'll probably need to know if the hardware has been initialized. And if it has been, we might also want to know the length of the running countdown.

Some device drivers create more than one software device. This is a purely logical device that is implemented over the top of the basic peripheral hardware. For example, it is easy to imagine that more than one software timer could be created from a single timer/counter unit. The timer/counter unit would be configured to generate a periodic clock tick, and the device driver would then manage a set of software timers of various lengths by maintaining state information for each.

3. A routine to initialize the hardware to a known state

Once you know how you'll track the state of the physical and logical devices, it's time to start writing the functions that actually interact with and control the device. It is probably best to begin with the hardware initialization routine. You'll need that one first anyway, and it's a good way to get familiar with the device interaction.

4. A set of routines that, taken together, provide an API for users of the device driver

After you've successfully initialized the device, you can start adding other functionality to the driver. Hopefully, you've already settled on the names and purposes of the various routines, as well as their respective parameters and return values. All that's left to do now is implement and test each one. We'll see examples of such routines in the next section.

5. One or more interrupt service routines

It's best to design, implement, and test most of the device driver routines before enabling interrupts for the first time. Locating the source of interrupt-related problems can be quite challenging. And, if you add possible bugs in the other driver modules to the mix, it could even approach impossible. It's far better to use polling to get the guts of the driver working. That way you'll know how the device works (and that it is indeed working) when you start looking for the source of your interrupt problems. And there will almost certainly be some of those.

A Simple Timer Driver

The device driver example that we're about to discuss is designed to control one of the timer/counter units contained within the 80188EB processor. I have chosen to implement this driver—and all of the remaining examples in the book—in C++. Although C++ offers no additional assistance over C in accessing hardware registers, there are many good reasons to use it for this type of abstraction. Most notably, C++ classes allow us to hide the actual hardware interface more completely than any C features or programming techniques. For example, a constructor can be included to automatically configure the hardware each time a new timer object is declared. This eliminates the need for an explicit call from the application software to the driver initialization routine. In addition, it is possible to hide the data structure that corresponds to the device registers within the private part of the associated class. This helps to prevent the application programmer from accidentally reading or writing the device registers from some other part of the program.

The definition of the **Timer** class is as follows:

```
enum TimerState { Idle, Active, Done };
enum TimerType  { OneShot, Periodic };

class Timer
{
    public:

        Timer();
        ~Timer();

        int    start(unsigned int nMilliseconds, TimerType = OneShot);
        int    waitfor();
        void   cancel();

        TimerState     state;
        TimerType      type;
        unsigned int   length;

        unsigned int   count;
        Timer *        pNext;

    private:

        static void interrupt  Interrupt();
};
```

Before discussing the implementation of this class, let's examine the previous declaration and consider the device driver's overall structure. The first thing we see are two enumerated types, `TimerState` and `TimerType`. The main purpose of these types is to make the rest of the code more readable. From them we learn that each software timer has a current state—`Idle`, `Active`, or `Done`—and a type—`OneShot` or `Periodic`. The timer's type tells the driver what to do with the timer when it expires; a `Periodic` timer is to be restarted then.

The constructor for the `Timer` class is also the device driver's initialization routine. It ensures that the timer/counter hardware is actively generating a clock tick every 1 millisecond. The other public methods of the class—*start, waitfor,* and *cancel*—provide an API for an easy-to-use software timer. These methods allow application programmers to start one-shot and periodic timers, wait for them to expire, and cancel running timers, respectively. This is a much simpler and more generic interface than that provided by the timer/counter hardware within the 80188EB chip. For one thing, the timer hardware does not know about human units of time, like milliseconds. But because the timer driver hides the specifics of this particular hardware, the application programmer need never even know about that.

The data members of the class should also help give you some insight into the device driver implementation. The first three items are variables that answer the following questions about this software timer:

- What is the timer's current state (idle, active, or done)?

- What type of a timer is it (one-shot or periodic)?

- What is the total length of the timer (in units called ticks)?

Following those are two more data members, both of which contain information that is specific to this implementation of the timer driver. The values of `count` and `pNext` have meaning only within the context of a linked list of active software timers. This linked list is ordered by the number of ticks remaining for each timer. So `count` contains information about the number of ticks remaining before this software timer is set to expire,[*] and `pNext` is a pointer to the software timer that will expire the soonest after this one.

Finally, there is a private method called *Interrupt*—our interrupt service routine. The *Interrupt* method is declared `static` because it is not allowed to manipulate the data members of the individual software timers. So, for example, the interrupt service routine is not allowed to modify the `state` of any timer. By using the keyword `static`, this restriction is automatically enforced for us by the C++ compiler.

---

[*] Specifically, it represents the number of clock ticks remaining after all of the timers ahead of it in the list have expired.

The most important thing to learn from the class declaration is that, although all of the software timers are driven by the same hardware timer/counter unit, each has its own private data store. This allows the application programmer to create multiple simultaneous software timers and the device driver to manage them behind the scenes. Once you grasp that idea, you're ready to look at the implementation of the driver's initialization routine, API, and interrupt service routine.

The constructor for the **Timer** class is responsible for initializing both the software timer and the underlying hardware. With respect to the latter, it is responsible for configuring the timer/counter unit, inserting the address of the interrupt service routine into the interrupt vector table, and enabling timer interrupts. However, because this method is a constructor that may be called several times (once for each of the **Timer** objects declared), our implementation of the constructor must be smart enough to perform these hardware initializations only during the very first call to it. Otherwise, the timer/counter unit might be reset at an inopportune time or become out of sync with the device driver.

That is the reason for the static variable **bInitialized** in the following code. This variable is declared with an initial value of zero and set to one after the hardware initialization sequence has been performed. Subsequent calls to the *Timer* constructor will see that **bInitialized** is no longer zero and skip that part of the initialization sequence.

```
#include "i8018xEB.h"
#include "timer.h"

#define CYCLES_PER_TICK   (25000/4)        // Number of clock cycles per tick.

/************************************************************************
 *
 * Method:       Timer()
 *
 * Description: Constructor for the Timer class.
 *
 * Notes:
 *
 * Returns:      None defined.
 *
 ************************************************************************/
Timer::Timer(void)
{
    static int bInitialized = 0;


    //
    // Initialize the new software timer.
    //
    state  = Idle;
    type   = OneShot;
    length = 0;
```

```
        count  = 0;
        pNext  = NULL;

        //
        // Initialize the timer hardware, if not previously done.
        //
        if (!bInitialized)
        {
            //
            // Install the interrupt handler and enable timer interrupts.
            //
            gProcessor.installHandler(TIMER2_INT, Timer::Interrupt);
            gProcessor.pPCB->intControl.timerControl &=
                                ~(TIMER_MASK | TIMER_PRIORITY);


            //
            // Initialize the hardware device (use Timer #2).
            //
            gProcessor.pPCB->timer[2].count = 0;
            gProcessor.pPCB->timer[2].maxCountA = CYCLES_PER_TICK;
            gProcessor.pPCB->timer[2].control = TIMER_ENABLE
                                    | TIMER_INTERRUPT
                                    | TIMER_PERIODIC;


            //
            // Mark the timer hardware initialized.
            //
            bInitialized = 1;
        }
    }   /* Timer() */
```

The global object **gProcessor** is declared in a header file called *i8018xEB.h*. It represents the Intel 80188EB processor. The **i8018xEB** class is something that I wrote, and it includes methods to make interaction with the processor and its on-chip peripherals easier. One of these methods is called *installHandler*, and its job is to insert an interrupt service routine into the interrupt vector table. This class also includes a global data structure called **PCB** that can be overlaid upon the memory-mapped registers of the peripheral control block.* The three registers associated with timer/counter unit 2 make up just one small part of this 256-byte structure. (For purely aesthetic reasons, I've implemented the PCB data structure as a set of nested structures. Hence, the control register of timer/counter unit 2 is accessible as **pPCB->timer[2].control**.)

The initialization of the timer/counter unit consists of resetting its **count** register to 0, loading the **maxCountA** register with the countdown length, and setting several

---

* Astute readers might recall that in Chapter 5, *Getting to Know the Hardware*, I stated that the PCB was located in the I/O space of the 80188EB processor. However, because memory-mapped registers are more likely in a device driver situation, I've relocated the entire PCB to physical address 72000h, in the memory space. This new location will be assumed for the rest of the book. To see how this relocation was performed, take a look at the constructor for the i8018xEB class.

bits within the `control` register. What we are doing above is starting a 1 ms periodic timer that generates an interrupt at the end of each cycle. (This periodic timer will act as the clock tick we need to create software timers of arbitrary lengths.) The value that is loaded into `maxCountA` can be determined mathematically because it represents the number of clock cycles input to the timer/counter unit in a 1 ms period. According to the 80188EB databook, this will be one fourth of the number of processor cycles in a 1 ms period. So, for a 25 MHz processor like the one we're using (that's 25,000,000 cycles per second, or, if you prefer, 25,000 cycles per millisecond), `maxCountA` should be set to 25,000/4—as it is in the constant `CYCLES_PER_TICK` earlier.

Once the hardware has been initialized and the clock tick established, it is possible to start a software timer of any length, so long as that length can be expressed as an integral number of ticks. Because our clock tick is 1 ms long, the application programmer can create timers of any length from 1 to 65,535 ms (65.536 seconds). He would do this by calling the *start* method:

```
/*********************************************************************
 *
 * Method:       start()
 *
 * Description: Start a software timer, based on the tick from the
 *              underlying hardware timer.
 *
 * Notes:
 *
 * Returns:      0 on success, -1 if the timer is already in use.
 *
 *********************************************************************/
int
Timer::start(unsigned int nMilliseconds, TimerType timerType)
{
    if (state != Idle)
    {
        return (-1);
    }

    //
    // Initialize the software timer.
    //
    state  = Active;
    type   = timerType;
    length = nMilliseconds / MS_PER_TICK;

    //
    // Add this timer to the active timer list.
    //
    timerList.insert(this);

    return (0);

}   /* start() */
```

When a software timer is started, the data members `state`, `type`, and `length` are initialized and the timer is inserted into a linked list of active timers called the `timerList`. The timers in the timer list are ordered so that the first timer to expire is at the top of the list. In addition, each timer has a `count` associated with it. This value represents the number of ticks that will be remaining in the software timer once all previous timers in the list have expired. Taken together, these design choices favor quick updates to the timer list at the price of slower insertions and deletions. Speed is important during updates because the timer list will be updated every time the hardware generates a clock tick interrupt—that's every one millisecond.

Figure 7-1 shows the timer list in action. Remember that each software timer has its own unique length and starting time, but once it has been inserted into the list, only the `count` field matters for ordering. In the example shown, the first and second timers were both started (the second might actually have been restarted, because it is periodic) at the same time. Since the second is 5 ms longer, it will expire 5 clock ticks after the first. The second and third timers in the list both happen to expire at the same time, though the third timer will have been running for 10 times longer.

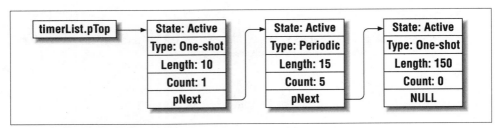

Figure 7-1. The timer list in action

The code for the interrupt service routine is shown below. This routine is declared to be of type `void interrupt`. The keyword `interrupt` is an extension of the C/C++ language that is understood only by compilers for 80x86 processors. By declaring the routine in this way, we ask the compiler to save and restore all of the processor's registers at the entry and exit, rather than only those that are saved during an ordinary function call.

```
/*********************************************************************
 *
 * Method:      Interrupt()
 *
 * Description: An interrupt handler for the timer hardware.
 *
 * Notes:       This method is declared static, so that we cannot
 *              inadvertently modify any of the software timers.
 *
 * Returns:     None defined.
 *
 *********************************************************************/
```

```
void interrupt
Timer::Interrupt()
{
    //
    // Decrement the active timer's count.
    //
    timerList.tick();

    //
    // Acknowledge the timer interrupt.
    //
    gProcessor.pPCB->intControl.eoi = EOI_NONSPECIFIC;

    //
    // Clear the Maximum Count bit (to start the next cycle).
    //
    gProcessor.pPCB->timer[2].control &= ~TIMER_MAXCOUNT;

}   /* Interrupt() */
```

Of course, the *tick* method of the **TimerList** class does most of the work here. This method is mostly concerned with linked list manipulation and is not very exciting to look at. Briefly stated, the *tick* method starts by decrementing the tick count of the timer at the top of the list. If that timer's **count** has reached zero, it changes the state of the software timer to **Done** and removes it from the timer list. It also does the same for any timers that are set to expire on the very same tick. These are the ones at the new head of the list that also have a count of zero.

After creating and starting a software timer, the application programmer can do some other processing and then check to see if the timer has expired. The *waitfor* method is provided for that purpose. This routine will block until the software timer's state is changed to **Done** by *timerList.tick*. The implementation of this method is as follows:

```
/************************************************************************
 *
 * Method:      waitfor()
 *
 * Description: Wait for the software timer to finish.
 *
 * Notes:
 *
 * Returns:     0 on success, -1 if the timer is not running.
 *
 ************************************************************************/
int
Timer::waitfor()
{
    if (state != Active)
    {
        return (-1);
    }
```

```
    //
    // Wait for the timer to expire.
    //
    while (state != Done);

    //
    // Restart or idle the timer, depending on its type.
    //
    if (type == Periodic)
    {
        state = Active;
        timerList.insert(this);
    }
    else
    {
        state = Idle;
    }

    return (0);

}   /* waitfor() */
```

One important thing to notice about this code is that the test `while (state !=
Done)` is not an infinite loop. That's because, as we just learned a few paragraphs
back, the timer's state is modified by *timerList.tick*, which is called from the interrupt service routine. In fact, if we were being careful embedded programmers, we
would have declared `state` as `volatile`. Doing so would prevent the compiler
from incorrectly assuming that the timer's state is either done or not done and
optimizing away the while loop.[*]

The final method of the `Timer` class is used to cancel a running timer. This is easy
to implement because we need only remove the timer from the timer list and
change its state to `Idle`. The code that actually does this is shown here:

```
/********************************************************************
 *
 * Method:      cancel()
 *
 * Description: Stop a running timer.
 *
 * Notes:
 *
 * Returns:     None defined.
 *
 ********************************************************************/
void
```

---

[*] A word of caution about *waitfor*: this implementation spins its wheels waiting for the software timer to
change to the done state. This technique is called busy-waiting, and it is neither elegant nor an efficient
use of the processor. In Chapter 8, *Operating Systems*, we'll see how the introduction of an operating system allows us to improve upon this implementation.

```
Timer::cancel(void)
{
    //
    // Remove the timer from the timer list.
    //
    if (state == Active)
    {
        timerList.remove(this);
    }

    //
    // Reset the timer's state.
    //
    state = Idle;

}   /* cancel() */
```

Of course, there is also a destructor for the **Timer** class, though I won't show the code here. Suffice it to say that it just checks to see if the software timer is active and, if so, removes it from the timer list. This prevents a periodic timer that has gone out of scope from remaining in the timer list indefinitely and any pointers to the "dead" timer from remaining in the system.

For completeness, it might be nice to add a public method, perhaps called *poll*, that allows users of the **Timer** class to test the state of a software timer without blocking. In the interest of space, I have left this out of my implementation, but it would be easy to add such a routine. It need only return the current value of the comparison **state == Done**. However, in order to do this, some technique would need to be devised to restart periodic timers for which *waitfor* is never called.

Another potential feature of the **Timer** class is asynchronous callbacks. In other words, why not allow the creator of a software timer to attach a function to it. This function could then be called automatically—via *timerList.tick*—each time that timer expires. As you read the next section, be sure to think about how different the Blinking LED program would look if asynchronous callbacks were used instead. This is one type of application to which asynchronous function calls are particularly well suited.

Das Blinkenlights, Revisited

Now that we have the **Timer** class at our disposal, it is possible to rewrite the book's very first example to make its timing more precise. Recall that in our original implementation, we relied on the fact that the length of a "decrement and compare" operation was fixed for a given processor and speed. We simply took a guess as to how long that might be and then revised our estimate based on empirical testing. By utilizing the **Timer** class, we can simultaneously eliminate this guesswork and increase the readability of the program.

Watchdog Timers

Another type of timer you might hear mentioned frequently in reference to embedded systems is a watchdog timer. This is a special piece of hardware that protects the system from software hangs. If present, the watchdog timer is always counting down from some large number to zero. This process typically takes a few seconds to complete. In the meantime, it is possible for the embedded software to "kick" the watchdog timer, to reset its counter to the original large number. If the counter ever does reach zero, the watchdog timer will assume that the software is hung. It then resets the embedded processor and, thus, restarts the software.

This is a common way to recover from unexpected software hangs that occur after the system is deployed. For example, suppose that your company's new product will travel into space. No matter how much testing you do before deployment, the possibility remains that there are undiscovered bugs lurking in the software and that one or more of these is capable of hanging the system altogether. If the software hangs, you won't be able to communicate with it at all, so you can't just issue a reset command remotely. Instead, you must build an automatic recovery mechanism into the system. And that's where the watchdog timer comes in.

The implementation of the watchdog timer "kick" would look just like the Blinking LED program in this chapter, except that instead of toggling the LED the watchdog timer's counter would be reset.

In the revised Blinking LED program below you will see that we can now simply start a periodic 500 ms software timer, toggle the LED, and then wait for the timer to expire before toggling the LED again. In the meantime, we could perform other processing tasks required by the application at hand.

```
#include "timer.h"
#include "led.h"

/*********************************************************************
 *
 * Function:    main()
 *
 * Description: Blink the green LED once a second.
 *
 * Notes:       This outer loop is hardware-independent.  However, it
 *              calls the hardware-dependent function toggleLed().
 *
 * Returns:     This routine contains an infinite loop.
 *
 *********************************************************************/
```

```
void
main(void)
{
    Timer  timer;

    timer.start(500, Periodic);      // Start a periodic 500 ms timer.

    while (1)
    {
        toggleLed(LED_GREEN);        // Toggle the green LED.

        // Do other useful work here.

        timer.waitfor();             // Wait for the timer to expire.
    }

}   /* main() */
```

8

In this chapter:
- *History and Purpose*
- *A Decent Embedded Operating System*
- *Real-Time Characteristics*
- *Selection Process*

Operating Systems

o•s•o•pho•bi•a n. A common fear among embedded systems programmers.

All but the most trivial of embedded programs will benefit from the inclusion of an operating system. This can range from a small kernel written by you to a full-featured commercial operating system. Either way, you'll need to know what features are the most important and how their implementation will affect the rest of your software. At the very least, you need to understand what an embedded operating system looks like on the outside. But there's probably no better way to understand the exterior interfaces than to examine a small operating system in its entirety. So that's what we'll do in this chapter.

History and Purpose

In the early days of computing there was no such thing as an operating system. Application programmers were completely responsible for controlling and monitoring the state of the processor and other hardware. In fact, the purpose of the first operating systems was to provide a virtual hardware platform that made application programs easier to write. To accomplish this goal, operating system developers needed only provide a loose collection of routines—much like a modern software library—for resetting the hardware to a known state, reading the state of the inputs, and changing the state of the outputs.

Modern operating systems add to this the ability to execute multiple software tasks simultaneously on a single processor. Each such task is a piece of the software that can be separated from and run independently of the rest. A set of embedded software requirements can usually be decomposed into a small number of such independent pieces. For example, the printer-sharing device described in Chapter 5, *Getting to Know the Hardware*, contains three obvious software tasks:

- Task 1: Receive data from the computer attached to serial port A.

- Task 2: Receive data from the computer attached to serial port B.

- Task 3: Format and send the waiting data (if any) to the printer attached to the parallel port.

Tasks provide a key software abstraction that makes the design and implementation of embedded software easier and the resulting source code simpler to understand and maintain. By breaking the larger program up into smaller pieces, the programmer can more easily concentrate her energy and talents on the unique features of the system under development.

Strictly speaking, an operating system is not a required component of any computer system—embedded or otherwise. It is always possible to perform the same functions from within the application program itself. Indeed, all of the examples so far in this book have done just that. There is simply one path of execution—starting at *main*—that is downloaded into the system and run. This is the equivalent of having only one task. But as the complexity of the application expands beyond just blinking an LED, the benefits of an operating system far outweigh the associated costs.

If you have never worked on operating system internals before, you might have the impression that they are complex. I'm sure the operating system vendors would like you to continue to believe that they are and that only a handful of computer scientists are capable of writing one. But I'm here to let the cat out of the bag: it's not all that hard! In fact, embedded operating systems are even easier to write than their desktop cousins—the required functionality is smaller and better defined. Once you learn what that functionality is and a few implementation techniques, you will see that an operating system is no harder to develop than any other piece of embedded software.

Embedded operating systems are small because they lack many of the things you would expect to find on your desktop computer. For example, embedded systems rarely have disk drives or graphical displays, and hence they need no filesystem or graphical user interface in their operating systems. In addition, there is only one "user" (i.e., all of the tasks that comprise the embedded software cooperate), so the security features of multiuser operating systems do not apply. All of these are features that could be part of an embedded operating system but are unnecessary in the majority of cases.

A Decent Embedded Operating System

What follows is a description of an embedded operating system that I have developed on my own. I call my operating system ADEOS (pronounced the same as the

Spanish farewell), which is an acronym for "A Decent Embedded Operating System." I think that name really sums it up nicely. Yes, it is an embedded operating system; but it is neither the best nor the worst in any regard. In all, there are less than 1000 lines of source code. Of these, three quarters are platform-independent and written in C++. The rest are hardware- or processor-specific and, therefore, written in assembly language. In the discussion later, I will present and explain all of the routines that are written in C++ along with the theory you need to understand them. In the interest of clarity, I will not present the source code for the assembly language routines. Instead, I will simply state their purpose and assume that interested readers will download and examine that code on their own.

If you would like to use ADEOS (or a modified version of it) in your embedded system, please feel free to do so. In fact, I would very much like to hear from anyone who uses it. I have made every effort to test the code and improve upon the weaknesses I have uncovered. However, I can make no guarantee that the code presented in this chapter is useful for any purpose other than learning about operating systems. If you decide to use it anyway, please be prepared to spend some amount of your time finding and fixing bugs in the operating system itself.

Tasks

We have already talked about multitasking and the idea that an operating system makes it possible to execute multiple "programs" at the same time. But what does that mean? How is it possible to execute several tasks concurrently? In actuality, the tasks are not executed at the same time. Rather, they are executed in pseudoparallel. They merely take turns using the processor. This is similar to the way several people might read the same copy of a book. Only one person can actually use the book at a given moment, but they can both read it by taking turns using it.

An operating system is responsible for deciding which task gets to use the processor at a particular moment. In addition, it maintains information about the state of each task. This information is called the task's context, and it serves a purpose similar to a bookmark. In the multiple book reader scenario, each reader is presumed to have her own bookmark. The bookmark's owner must be able to recognize it (e.g., it has her name written on it), and it must indicate where she stopped reading when last she gave up control of the book. This is the reader's context.

A task's context records the state of the processor just prior to another task's taking control of it. This usually consists of a pointer to the next instruction to be executed (the instruction pointer), the address of the current top of the stack (the stack pointer), and the contents of the processor's flag and general-purpose registers. On 16-bit 80x86 processors, these are the registers CS and IP, SS and SP, Flags, and DS, ES, SI, DI, AX, BX, CX, and DX, respectively.

In order to keep tasks and their contexts organized, the operating system maintains a bit of information about each task. Operating systems written in C often keep this information in a data structure called the task control block. However, ADEOS is written in C++ and one of the advantages of this approach is that the task-specific data is automatically made a part of the task object itself. The definition of a `Task`, which includes the information that the operating system needs, is as follows:

```
class Task
{
    public:

        Task(void (*function)(), Priority p, int stackSize);

        TaskId          id;
        Context         context;
        TaskState       state;
        Priority        priority;
        int *           pStack;
        Task *          pNext;

        void  (*entryPoint)();

    private:

        static TaskId  nextId;
};
```

Many of the data members of this class will make sense only after we discuss the operating system in greater detail. However, the first two fields—id and `context`—should already sound familiar. The `id` contains a unique integer (between 0 and 255) that identifies the task. In other words, it is the name on the bookmark. The `context` is the processor-specific data structure that actually contains the state of the processor the last time this task gave up control of the processor.

Task states

Remember how I said that only one task could actually be using the processor at a given time? That task is said to be the "running" task, and no other task can be in that same state at the same time. Tasks that are ready to run—but are not currently using the processor—are in the "ready" state, and tasks that are waiting for some event external to themselves to occur before going on are in the "waiting" state. Figure 8-1 shows the relationships between these three states.

A transition between the ready and running states occurs whenever the operating system selects a new task to run. The task that was previously running becomes ready, and the new task (selected from the pool of tasks in the ready state) is promoted to running. Once it is running, a task will leave that state only if it is forced

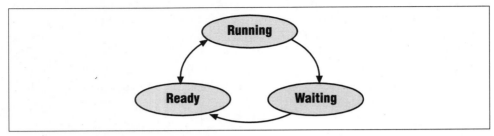

Figure 8-1. Possible states of a task

to do so by the operating system or if it needs to wait for some event external to itself to occur before continuing. In the latter case, the task is said to block, or wait, until that event occurs. And when that happens, the task enters the waiting state and the operating system selects one of the ready tasks to be run. So, although there may be any number of tasks in each of the ready and waiting states, there will never be more (or less) than one task in the running state at any time.

Here's how a task's state is actually defined in ADEOS:

```
enum TaskState { Ready, Running, Waiting };
```

It is important to note that only the scheduler—the part of the operating system that decides which task to run—can promote a task to the running state. Newly created tasks and tasks that are finished waiting for their external event are placed into the ready state first. The scheduler will then include these new ready tasks in its future decision-making.

Task mechanics

As an application developer working with ADEOS (or any other operating system), you will need to know how to create and use tasks. Like any other abstract data type, the `Task` class has its own set of routines to do just that. However, the task interface in ADEOS is simpler than most because you can do nothing but create new `Task` objects. Once created, an ADEOS task will continue to exist in the system until the associated function returns. Of course, that might not happen at all, but if it does, the task will be deleted automatically by the operating system.

The *Task* constructor is shown below. The caller assigns a function, a priority, and an optional stack size to the new task by way of the constructor's parameters. The first parameter, `function`, is a pointer to the C/C++ or assembly language function that is to be executed within the context of the new task. The only requirements for this function are that it take no arguments and return nothing. The second parameter, `p`, is a unique number from 1 to 255 that represents the new task's priority relative to other tasks in the system. These numbers are used by the scheduler when it is selecting the next task to be run (higher numbers represent higher priorities).

```
TaskId     Task::nextId = 0;

/*********************************************************************
 *
 * Method:       Task()
 *
 * Description: Create a new task and initialize its state.
 *
 * Notes:
 *
 * Returns:
 *
 *********************************************************************/
Task::Task(void (*function)(), Priority p, int stackSize)
{
    stackSize /= sizeof(int);                // Convert bytes to words.

    enterCS();                               ////// Critical Section Begin

    //
    // Initialize the task-specific data.
    //
    id          = Task::nextId++;
    state       = Ready;
    priority    = p;
    entryPoint  = function;
    pStack      = new int[stackSize];
    pNext       = NULL;

    //
    // Initialize the processor context.
    //
    contextInit(&context, run, this, pStack + stackSize);

    //
    // Insert the task into the ready list.
    //
    os.readyList.insert(this);

    os.schedule();                           // Scheduling Point

    exitCS();                                ////// Critical Section End

}   /* Task() */
```

Notice how the functional part of this routine is surrounded by the two function calls *enterCS* and *exitCS*. The block of code between these calls is said to be a *critical section*. A critical section is a part of a program that must be executed atomically. That is, the instructions that make up that part must be executed in order and without interruption. Because an interrupt can occur at any time, the only way to make such a guarantee is to disable interrupts for the duration of the critical section. So *enterCS* is called at the beginning of the critical section to save the interrupt enable state and disable further interrupts. And *exitCS* is called at the end to restore the previously saved interrupt state. We will see this same technique used in each of the routines that follow.

There are several other routines that I've called from the constructor in the previous code, but I don't have the space to list here. These are the routines *contextInit* and *os.readyList.insert*. The *contextInit* routine establishes the initial context for a task. This routine is necessarily processor-specific and, therefore, written in assembly language.

contextInit has four parameters. The first is a pointer to the context data structure that is to be initialized. The second is a pointer to the startup function. This is a special ADEOS function, called *run*, that is used to start a task and clean up behind it if the associated function later exits. The third parameter is a pointer to the new **Task** object. This parameter is passed to *run* so the function associated with the task can be started. The fourth and final parameter is a pointer to the new task's stack.

The other function call is to *os.readyList.insert*. This call adds the new task to the operating system's internal list of ready tasks. The **readyList** is an object of type **TaskList**. This class is just a linked list of tasks (ordered by priority) that has two methods: *insert* and *remove*. Interested readers should download and examine the source code for ADEOS if they want to see the actual implementation of these functions. You'll also learn more about the ready list in the discussion that follows.

Scheduler

The heart and soul of any operating system is its scheduler. This is the piece of the operating system that decides which of the ready tasks has the right to use the processor at a given time. If you've written software for a mainstream operating system, then you might be familiar with some of the more common scheduling algorithms: first-in-first-out, shortest job first, and round robin. These are simple scheduling algorithms that are used in nonembedded systems.

First-in-first-out (FIFO) scheduling describes an operating system like DOS, which is not a multitasking operating system at all. Rather, each task runs until it is finished, and only after that is the next task started. However, in DOS a task can suspend itself, thus freeing up the processor for the next task. And that's precisely how older version of the Windows operating system permitted users to switch from one task to another. True multitasking wasn't a part of any Microsoft operating system before Windows NT.

Application Programming Interfaces

One of the most annoying things about embedded operating systems is their lack of a common API. This is a particular problem for companies that want to share application code between products that are based on different operating systems. One company I worked for even went so far as to create their own layer above the operating system solely to isolate their application programmers from these differences. But surely this was just adding to the overall problem—by creating yet another API.

The basic functionality of every embedded operating system is much the same. Each function or method represents a service that the operating system can perform for the application program. But there aren't that many different services possible. And it is frequently the case that the only real difference between two implementations is the name of the function or method.

This problem has persisted for several decades, and there is no end in sight. Yet during that same time the Win32 and POSIX APIs have taken hold on PCs and Unix workstations, respectively. So why hasn't a similar standard emerged for embedded systems? It hasn't been for a lack of trying. In fact, the authors of the original POSIX standard (IEEE 1003.1) also created a standard for real-time systems (IEEE 1003.4b). And a few of the more Unix-like embedded operating systems (VxWorks and LynxOS come to mind) are compliant with this standard API. However, for the vast majority of application programmers, it is necessary to learn a new API for each operating system used.

Fortunately, there is a glimmer of hope. The Java programming language has support for multitasking and task synchronization built in. That means that no matter what operating system a Java program is running on, the mechanics of creating and manipulating tasks and synchronizing their activities remain the same. For this and several other reasons, Java would be a very nice language for embedded programmers. I hope that there will some day be a need for a book about embedded systems programming in Java and that a sidebar like this one will, therefore, no longer be required.

Shortest job first describes a similar scheduling algorithm. The only difference is that each time the running task completes or suspends itself, the next task selected is the one that will require the least amount of processor time to complete. Shortest job first was common on early mainframe systems because it has the appealing property of maximizing the number of satisfied customers. (Only the customers who have the longest jobs tend to notice or complain.)

Round robin is the only scheduling algorithm of the three in which the running task can be preempted, that is, interrupted while it is running. In this case, each task runs for some predetermined amount of time. After that time interval has elapsed, the running task is preempted by the operating system and the next task in line gets its chance to run. The preempted task doesn't get to run again until all of the other tasks have had their chances in that round.

Unfortunately, embedded operating systems cannot use any of these simplistic scheduling algorithms. Embedded systems (particularly real-time systems) almost always require a way to share the processor that allows the most important tasks to grab control of the processor as soon as they need it. Therefore, most embedded operating systems utilize a priority-based scheduling algorithm that supports preemption. This is a fancy way of saying that at any given moment the task that is currently using the processor is guaranteed to be the highest-priority task that is ready to do so. Lower-priority tasks must wait until higher-priority tasks are finished using the processor before resuming their work. The word preemptive adds that any running task can be interrupted by the operating system if a task of higher priority becomes ready. The scheduler detects such conditions at a finite set of time instants called scheduling points.

When a priority-based scheduling algorithm is used, it is also necessary to have a backup policy. This is the scheduling algorithm to be used in the event that several ready tasks have the same priority. The most common backup scheduling algorithm is round robin. However, for simplicity's sake, I've implemented only a FIFO scheduler for my backup policy. For that reason, users of ADEOS should take care to assign a unique priority to each task whenever possible. This shouldn't be a problem though, because ADEOS supports as many priority levels as tasks (up to 255 of each).

The scheduler in ADEOS is implemented in a class called `Sched`:

```
class Sched
{
    public:

        Sched();

        void  start();
        void  schedule();

        void  enterIsr();
        void  exitIsr();

        static Task *    pRunningTask;
        static TaskList  readyList;

        enum SchedState { Uninitialized, Initialized, Started };

    private:
```

```
            static SchedState  state;
            static Task        idleTask;
            static int         interruptLevel;
            static int         bSchedule;
    };
```

After defining this class, an object of this type is instantiated within one of the operating system modules. That way, users of ADEOS need only link the file *sched.obj* to include an instance of the scheduler. This instance is called os and is declared as follows:

```
    extern Sched os;
```

References to this global variable can be made from within any part of the application program. But you'll soon see that only one such reference will be necessary per application.

Scheduling points

Simply stated, the scheduling points are the set of operating system events that result in an invocation of the scheduler. We have already encountered two such events: task creation and task deletion. During each of these events, the method *os.schedule* is called to select the next task to be run. If the currently executing task still has the highest priority of all the ready tasks, it will be allowed to continue using the processor. Otherwise, the highest priority ready task will be executed next. Of course, in the case of task deletion a new task is always selected: the currently running task is no longer ready, by virtue of the fact that it no longer exists!

A third scheduling point is called the clock tick. The clock tick is a periodic event that is triggered by a timer interrupt. The clock tick provides an opportunity to awake tasks that are waiting for a software timer to expire. This is almost exactly the same as the timer tick we saw in the previous chapter. In fact, support for software timers is a common feature of embedded operating systems. During the clock tick, the operating system decrements and checks each of the active software timers. When a timer expires, all of the tasks that are waiting for it to complete are changed from the waiting state to the ready state. Then the scheduler is invoked to see if one of these newly awakened tasks has a higher priority than the task that was running prior to the timer interrupt.

The clock tick routine in ADEOS is almost exactly the same as the one in Chapter 7, *Peripherals*. In fact, we still use the same Timer class. Only the implementation of this class has been changed, and that only slightly. These changes are meant to account for the fact that multiple tasks might be waiting for the same software timer. In addition, all of the calls to *disable* and *enable* have been replaced by *enterCS* and *exitCS,* and the length of a clock tick has been increased from 1 ms to 10 ms.

Ready list

The scheduler uses a data structure called the ready list to track the tasks that are in the ready state. In ADEOS, the ready list is implemented as an ordinary linked list, ordered by priority. So the head of this list is always the highest priority task that is ready to run. Following a call to the scheduler, this will be the same as the currently running task. In fact, the only time that won't be the case is during a reschedule. Figure 8-2 shows what the ready list might look like while the operating system is in use.

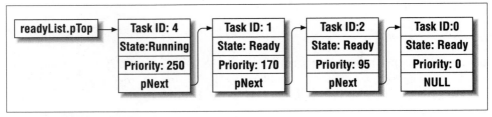

Figure 8-2. The ready list in action

The main advantage of an ordered linked list like this one is the ease with which the scheduler can select the next task to be run. (It's always at the top.) Unfortunately, there is a tradeoff between lookup time and insertion time. The lookup time is minimized because the data member `readyList` always points directly to the highest priority ready task. However, each time a new task changes to the ready state, the code within the *insert* method must walk down the ready list until it finds a task that has a lower priority than the one being inserted. The newly ready task is inserted in front of that task. As a result, the insertion time is proportional to the average number of tasks in the ready list.

Idle task

If there are no tasks in the ready state when the scheduler is called, the idle task will be executed. The idle task looks the same in every operating system. It is simply an infinite loop that does nothing. In ADEOS, the idle task is completely hidden from the application developer. It does, however, have a valid task ID and priority (both of which are zero, by the way). The idle task is always considered to be in the ready state (when it is not running), and because of its low priority, it will always be found at the end of the ready list. That way, the scheduler will find it automatically when there are no other tasks in the ready state. Those other tasks are sometimes referred to as user tasks to distinguish them from the idle task.

Scheduler

Because I use an ordered linked list to maintain the ready list, the scheduler is easy to implement. It simply checks to see if the running task and the highest-priority ready task are one and the same. If they are, the scheduler's job is done. Otherwise, it will initiate a context switch from the former task to the latter. Here's what this looks like when it's implemented in C++:

```cpp
/*********************************************************************
 *
 * Method:      schedule()
 *
 * Description: Select a new task to be run.
 *
 * Notes:       If this routine is called from within an ISR, the
 *              schedule will be postponed until the nesting level
 *              returns to zero.
 *
 *              The caller is responsible for disabling interrupts.
 *
 * Returns:     None defined.
 *
 ********************************************************************/
void
Sched::schedule(void)
{
    Task *  pOldTask;
    Task *  pNewTask;


    if (state != Started) return;

    //
    // Postpone rescheduling until all interrupts are completed.
    //
    if (interruptLevel != 0)
    {
        bSchedule = 1;
        return;
    }

    //
    // If there is a higher-priority ready task, switch to it.
    //
    if (pRunningTask != readyList.pTop)
    {
        pOldTask = pRunningTask;
        pNewTask = readyList.pTop;

        pNewTask->state = Running;
        pRunningTask = pNewTask;

        if (pOldTask == NULL)
```

```
        {
            contextSwitch(NULL, &pNewTask->context);
        }
        else
        {
            pOldTask->state = Ready;
            contextSwitch(&pOldTask->context, &pNewTask->context);
        }
    }

}    /* schedule() */
```

As you can see from this code, there are two situations during which the scheduler will not initiate a context switch. The first is if multitasking has not been
enabled. This is necessary because application programmers sometimes want to
create some or all of their tasks before actually starting the scheduler. In that case,
the application's *main* routine would look like the following one. Each time a
Task object is created, the scheduler is invoked.* However, because *schedule*
checks the value of state to ensure that multitasking has been started, no context switches will occur until after *start* is called.

```
#include "adeos.h"

void   taskAfunction(void);
void   taskBfunction(void);

/*
 * Create two tasks, each with its own unique function and priority.
 */
Task   taskA(taskAfunction, 150, 256);
Task   taskB(taskBfunction, 200, 256);

/********************************************************************
 *
 * Function:    main()
 *
 * Description: This is what an application program might look like
 *              if ADEOS were used as the operating system.  This
 *              function is responsible for starting the operating
 *              system only.
 *
 * Notes:       Any code placed after the call to os.start() will
 *              never be executed.  This is because main() is not a
 *              task, so it does not get a chance to run once the
 *              scheduler is started.
 *
 * Returns:     This function will never return!
 *
 ********************************************************************/
```

---

* Remember, task creation is one of our scheduling points. If the scheduler has been started, there is also
a possibility that the new task will be the highest priority ready task.

```
void
main(void)
{
    os.start();

    // This point will never be reached.

}   /* main() */
```

Because this is an important piece of code, let me reiterate what you are looking at. This is an example of the application code you might write as a user of ADEOS. You begin by including the header file *adeos.h* and declaring your tasks. After you declare the tasks and call *os.start*, the task functions *taskAfunction* and *taskBfunction* will begin to execute (in pseudoparallel). Of course, `taskB` has the highest priority of the two (200), so it will get to run first. However, as soon as it relinquishes control of the processor for any reason, the other task will have a chance to run as well.

The other situation in which the ADEOS scheduler will not perform a context switch is during interrupt processing. The operating system tracks the nesting level of the current interrupt service routine and allows context switches only if the nesting level is zero. If the scheduler is called from an ISR (as it is during the timer tick), the `bSchedule` flag is set to indicate that the scheduler should be called again as soon as the outermost interrupt handler exits. This delayed scheduling speeds up interrupt response times throughout the system.

Context Switch

The actual process of changing from one task to another is called a context switch. Because contexts are processor-specific, so is the code that implements the context switch. That means it must always be written in assembly language. Rather than show you the 80x86-specific assembly code that I used in ADEOS, I'll show the context switch routine in a C-like pseudocode:

```
void
contextSwitch(PContext pOldContext, PContext pNewContext)
{
    if (saveContext(pOldContext))
    {
        //
        // Restore new context only on a nonzero exit from saveContext().
        //
        restoreContext(pNewContext);

        // This line is never executed!
    }

    // Instead, the restored task continues to execute at this point.
}
```

The *contextSwitch* routine is actually invoked by the scheduler, which is in turn called from one of the operating system calls that disables interrupts. So it is not necessary to disable interrupts here. In addition, because the operating system call that invoked the scheduler is written in a high-level language, most of the running task's registers have already been saved onto its local stack. That reduces the amount of work that needs to be done by the routines *saveContext* and *restoreContext*. They need only worry about saving the instruction pointer, stack pointer, and flags.

The actual behavior of *contextSwitch* at runtime is difficult to see simply by looking at the previous code. Most software developers think serially, assuming that each line of code will be executed immediately following the previous one. However, this code is actually executed two times, in pseudoparallel. When one task (the new task) changes to the running state, another (the old task) must simultaneously go back to the ready state. Imagine what the new task sees when it is restored inside the *restoreContext* code. No matter what the new task was doing before, it always wakes up inside the *saveContext* code—because that's where its instruction pointer was saved.

How does the new task know whether it is coming out of *saveContext* for the first time (i.e., in the process of going to sleep) or the second time (in the process of waking up)? It definitely does need to know the difference, so I've had to implement *saveContext* in a slightly sneaky way. Rather than saving the precise current instruction pointer, *saveContext* actually saves an address a few instructions ahead. That way, when the saved context is restored, execution continues from a different point in the *saveContext* routine. This also makes it possible for *saveContext* to return different values: nonzero when the task goes to sleep and zero when the task wakes up. The *contextSwitch* routine uses this return value to decide whether to call *restoreContext*. If *contextSwitch* did not perform this check, the code associated with the new task would never get to execute.

I know this can be a complicated sequence of events to follow, so I've illustrated the whole process in Figure 8-3.

Task Synchronization

Though we frequently talk about the tasks in a multitasking operating system as completely independent entities, that portrayal is not completely accurate. All of the tasks are working together to solve a larger problem and must occasionally communicate with one another to synchronize their activities. For example, in the printer-sharing device the printer task doesn't have any work to do until new data is supplied to it by one of the computer tasks. So the printer and computer tasks must communicate with one another to coordinate their access to common data buffers. One way to do this is to use a data structure called a mutex.

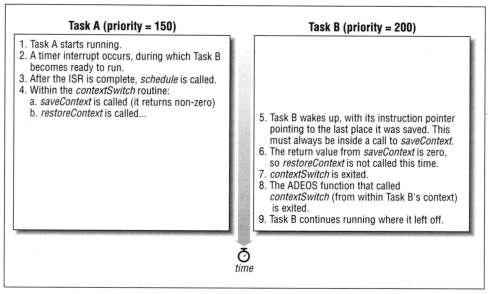

Task A (priority = 150)

1. Task A starts running.
2. A timer interrupt occurs, during which Task B becomes ready to run.
3. After the ISR is complete, *schedule* is called.
4. Within the *contextSwitch* routine:
   a. *saveContext* is called (it returns non-zero)
   b. *restoreContext* is called...

Task B (priority = 200)

5. Task B wakes up, with its instruction pointer pointing to the last place it was saved. This must always be inside a call to *saveContext*.
6. The return value from *saveContext* is zero, so *restoreContext* is not called this time.
7. *contextSwitch* is exited.
8. The ADEOS function that called *contextSwitch* (from within Task B's context) is exited.
9. Task B continues running where it left off.

time

Figure 8-3. A context switch

Mutexes are provided by many operating systems to assist with task synchronization. They are not, however, the only such mechanism available. Others are called semaphores, message queues, and monitors. However, if you have any one of these data structures, it is possible to implement each of the others. In fact, a mutex is itself a special type of semaphore called a binary, or mutual-exclusion, semaphore.

You can think of a mutex as being nothing more than a multitasking-aware binary flag. The meaning associated with a particular mutex must, therefore, be chosen by the software designer and understood by each of the tasks that use it. For example, the data buffer that is shared by the printer and computer task would probably have a mutex associated with it. When this binary flag is set, the shared data buffer is assumed to be in use by one of the tasks. All other tasks must wait until that flag is cleared (and then set again by themselves) before reading or writing any of the data within that buffer.

We say that mutexes are multitasking-aware because the processes of setting and clearing the binary flag are atomic. That is, these operations cannot be interrupted. A task can safely change the state of the mutex without risking that a context switch will occur in the middle of the modification. If a context switch were to occur, the binary flag might be left in an unpredictable state and a deadlock between the tasks could result. The atomicity of the mutex set and clear operations is enforced by the operating system, which disables interrupts before reading or modifying the state of the binary flag.

ADEOS includes a **Mutex** class. Using this class, the application software can create and destroy mutexes, wait for a mutex to be cleared and then set it, or clear a mutex that was previously set. The last two operations are referred to as taking and releasing a mutex, respectively.

Here is the definition of the **Mutex** class:

```
class Mutex
{
    public:

        Mutex();

        void  take(void);
        void  release(void);

    private:

        TaskList  waitingList;

        enum { Available, Held } state;
};
```

The process of creating a new **Mutex** is simple. The following constructor will be executed automatically each time a new mutex object is instantiated:

```
/**********************************************************************
 *
 * Method:      Mutex()
 *
 * Description: Create a new mutex.
 *
 * Notes:
 *
 * Returns:
 *
 **********************************************************************/
Mutex::Mutex()
{
    enterCS();                             ////// Critical Section Begin

    state = Available;
    waitingList.pTop = NULL;

    exitCS();                              ////// Critical Section End

}   /* Mutex() */
```

All mutexes are created in the **Available** state and are associated with a linked list of waiting tasks that is initially empty. Of course, once you've created a mutex it is necessary to have some way to change its state, so the next method we'll discuss is *take*. This routine would typically be called by a task, before it reads or writes a shared resource. When the call to *take* returns, the calling task's exclusive access to that resource is guaranteed by the operating system. The code for this routine is as follows:

```
/********************************************************************
 *
 * Method:        take()
 *
 * Description: Wait for a mutex to become available, then take it.
 *
 * Notes:
 *
 * Returns:       None defined.
 *
 ********************************************************************/
void
Mutex::take(void)
{
    Task *  pCallingTask;


    enterCS();                          ////// Critical Section Begin

    if (state == Available)
    {
        //
        // The mutex is available.  Simply take it and return.
        //
        state = Held;
        waitingList.pTop = NULL;
    }
    else
    {
        //
        // The mutex is taken.  Add the calling task to the waiting list.
        //
        pCallingTask = os.pRunningTask;
        pCallingTask->state = Waiting;
        os.readyList.remove(pCallingTask);
        waitingList.insert(pCallingTask);

        os.schedule();                          // Scheduling Point

        // When the mutex is released, the caller begins executing here.
    }

    exitCS();                           ////// Critical Section End

}   /* take() */
```

The neatest thing about the *take* method is that if the mutex is currently held by another task (that is, the binary flag is already set), the calling task will be suspended until the mutex is released by that other task. This is kind of like telling your spouse that you are going to take a nap and asking him or her to wake you up when dinner is ready. It is even possible for multiple tasks to be waiting for the same mutex. In fact, the waiting list associated with each mutex is ordered by priority, so the highest-priority waiting task will always be awakened first.

The method that comes next is used to *release* a mutex. Although this method could be called by any task, it is expected that only a task that previously called *take* would invoke it. Unlike *take*, this routine will never block. However, one possible result of releasing the mutex could be to wake a task of higher priority. In that case, the releasing task would immediately be forced (by the scheduler) to give up control of the processor, in favor of the higher-priority task.

```
/************************************************************************
 *
 * Method:       release()
 *
 * Description: Release a mutex that is held by the calling task.
 *
 * Notes:
 *
 * Returns:      None defined.
 *
 ************************************************************************/
void
Mutex::release(void)
{
    Task *  pWaitingTask;


    enterCS();                              ////// Critical Section Begins

    if (state == Held)
    {
        pWaitingTask = waitingList.pTop;

        if (pWaitingTask != NULL)
        {
            //
            // Wake the first task on the waiting list.
            //
            waitingList.pTop = pWaitingTask->pNext;
            pWaitingTask->state = Ready;
            os.readyList.insert(pWaitingTask);

            os.schedule();                  // Scheduling Point
        }
        else
        {
```

```
            state = Available;
        }
    }

    exitCS();                        ////// Critical Section End

}   /* release() */
```

Critical sections

The primary use of mutexes is for the protection of shared resources. Shared resources are global variables, memory buffers, or device registers that are accessed by multiple tasks. A mutex can be used to limit access to such a resource to one task at a time. It is like the stoplight that controls access to an intersection. Remember that in a multitasking environment you generally don't know in which order the tasks will be executed at runtime. One task might be writing some data into a memory buffer when it is suddenly interrupted by a higher-priority task. If the higher-priority task were to modify that same region of memory, then bad things could happen. At the very least, some of the lower-priority task's data would be overwritten.

Pieces of code that access shared resources contain critical sections. We've already seen something similar inside the operating system. There, we simply disabled interrupts during the critical section. But tasks cannot (wisely) disable interrupts. If they were allowed to do so, other tasks—even higher-priority tasks that didn't share the same resource—would not be able to execute during that interval. So we want and need a mechanism to protect critical sections within tasks without disabling interrupts. And mutexes provide that mechanism.

You've now learned everything there is to learn about one simple embedded operating system. Its basic elements are the scheduler and scheduling points, context switch routine, definition of a task, and a mechanism for intertask communication. Every useful embedded operating system will have these same elements. However, you don't always need to know how they are implemented. You can usually just treat the operating system as a black box on which you, as application programmer, rely. You simply write the code for each task and make calls to the operating system when and if necessary. The operating system will ensure that these tasks run at the appropriate times relative to one another.

Real-Time Characteristics

Engineers often use the term *real-time* to describe computing problems for which a late answer is as bad as a wrong one. These problems are said to have deadlines, and embedded systems frequently operate under such constraints. For example, if the embedded software that controls your anti-lock brakes misses one of its

Deadlock and Priority Inversion

Mutexes are powerful tools for synchronizing access to shared resources. However, they are not without their own dangers. Two of the most important problems to watch out for are deadlock and priority inversion.

Deadlock can occur whenever there is a circular dependency between tasks and resources. The simplest example is that of two tasks, each of which require two mutexes: A and B. If one task takes mutex A and waits for mutex B while the other takes mutex B and waits for mutex A, then both tasks are waiting for an event that will never occur. This essentially brings both tasks to a halt and, though other tasks might continue to run for a while, could bring the entire system to a standstill eventually. The only way to end the deadlock is to reboot the entire system.

Priority inversion occurs whenever a higher-priority task is blocked, waiting for a mutex that is held by a lower-priority task. This might not sound like too big a deal—after all, the mutex is just doing its job of arbitrating access to the shared resource—because the higher-priority task is written with the knowledge that sometimes the lower-priority task will be using the resource they share. However, consider what happens if there is a third task that has a priority somewhere between those two.

This situation is illustrated in Figure 8-4. Here there are three tasks: high priority, medium priority, and low priority. Low becomes ready first (indicated by the rising edge) and, shortly thereafter, takes the mutex. Now, when high becomes ready, it must block (indicated by the shaded region) until low is done with their shared resource. The problem is that Medium, which does not even require access to that resource, gets to preempt Low and run even though it will delay High's use of the processor. Many solutions to this problem have been proposed, the most common of which is called "priority inheritance." This solution has Low's priority increased to that of High as soon as High begins waiting for the mutex. Some operating systems include this "fix" within their mutex implementation, but the majority do not.

deadlines, you might find yourself in an accident. (You might even be killed!) So it is extremely important that the designers of real-time embedded systems know everything they can about the behavior and performance of their hardware and software. In this section we will discuss the performance characteristics of real-time operating systems, which are a common component of real-time systems.

The designers of real-time systems spend a large amount of their time worrying about worst-case performance. They must constantly ask themselves questions like the following: What is the worst-case time between the human operator pressing

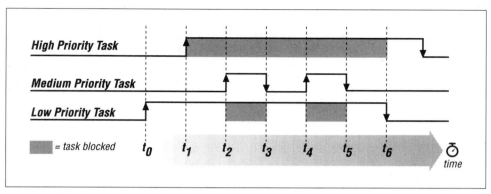

Figure 8-4. An example of priority inversion

the brake pedal and an interrupt signal arriving at the processor? What is the worst-case interrupt latency, the time between interrupt arrival and the start of the associated interrupt service routine (ISR)? And what is the worst-case time for the software to respond by triggering the braking mechanism? Average or expected-case analysis simply will not suffice in such systems.

Most of the commercial embedded operating systems available today are designed for possible inclusion in real-time systems. In the ideal case, this means that their worst-case performance is well understood and documented. To earn the distinctive title "Real-Time Operating System" (RTOS), an operating system should be deterministic and have guaranteed worst-case interrupt latency and context switch times. Given these characteristics and the relative priorities of the tasks and interrupts in your system, it is possible to analyze the worst-case performance of the software.

An operating system is said to be deterministic if the worst-case execution time of each of the system calls is calculable. An operating system vendor that takes the real-time behavior of its RTOS seriously will usually publish a data sheet that provides the minimum, average, and maximum number of clock cycles required by each system call. These numbers might be different for different processors, but it is reasonable to expect that if the algorithm is deterministic on one processor, it will be so on any other. (The actual times can differ.)

Interrupt latency is the total length of time from an interrupt signal's arrival at the processor to the start of the associated interrupt service routine. When an interrupt occurs, the processor must take several steps before executing the ISR. First, the processor must finish executing the current instruction. That probably takes less than one clock cycle, but some complex instructions require more time than that. Next, the interrupt type must be recognized. This is done by the processor hardware and does not slow or suspend the running task. Finally, and only if interrupts are enabled, the ISR that is associated with the interrupt is started.

Of course, if interrupts are ever disabled within the operating system, the worst-case interrupt latency increases by the maximum amount of time that they are turned off. But as we have just seen, there are many places where interrupts are disabled. These are the critical sections we talked about earlier, and there are no alternative methods for protecting them. Each operating system will disable interrupts for a different length of time, so it is important that you know what your system's requirements are. One real-time project might require a guaranteed interrupt response time as short as 1 μs, while another requires only 100 μs.

The third real-time characteristic of an operating system is the amount of time required to perform a context switch. This is important because it represents overhead across your entire system. For example, imagine that the average execution time of any task before it blocks is 100 μs but that the context switch time is also 100 μs. In that case, fully one-half of the processor's time is spent within the context switch routine! Again, there is no magic number and the actual times are usually processor-specific because they are dependent on the number of registers that must be saved and where. Be sure to get these numbers from any operating system vendor you are thinking of using. That way, there won't be any last-minute surprises.

Selection Process

Despite my earlier statement about how easy it is to write your own operating system, I still strongly recommend buying one if you can afford to. Let me say that again: I highly recommend buying a commercial operating system, rather than writing your own. I know of several good operating systems that can be obtained for just a few thousand dollars. Considering the cost of engineering time these days, that's a bargain by almost any measure. In fact, a wide variety of operating systems are available to suit most projects and pocketbooks. In this section we will discuss the process of selecting the commercial operating system that best fits the needs of your project.

Commercial operating systems form a continuum of functionality, performance, and price. Those at the lower end of the spectrum offer only a basic scheduler and a few other system calls. These operating systems are usually inexpensive, come with source code that you can modify, and do not require payment of royalties. Accelerated Technology's Nucleus and Kadak's AMX both fall into this category,* as do any of the embedded versions of DOS.

Operating systems at the other end of the spectrum typically include a lot of useful functionality beyond just the scheduler. They might also make stronger (or better)

---

* Please don't write to complain. I'm not maligning either of these operating systems. In fact, from what I know of both, I would highly recommend them as high-quality, low-cost commercial solutions.

guarantees about real-time performance. These operating systems can be quite expensive, though, with startup costs ranging from $10,000 to $50,000 and royalties due on every copy shipped in ROM. However, this price often includes free technical support and training and a set of integrated development tools. Examples are Wind River Systems' VxWorks, Integrated Systems' pSOS, and Microtec's VRTX. These are three of the most popular real-time operating systems on the market.

Between these two extremes are the operating systems that have a bit more functionality than just the basic scheduler and make some reasonable guarantees about their real-time performance. While the up-front costs and royalties are reasonable, these operating systems usually do not include source code, and technical support might cost extra. This is the category for most of the commercial operating systems not mentioned earlier.

With such a wide variety of operating systems and features to choose from, it can be difficult to decide which is the best for your project. Try putting your processor, real-time performance, and budgetary requirements first. These are criteria that you cannot change, so you can use them to narrow the possible choices to a dozen or fewer products. Then contact all of the vendors of the remaining operating systems for more detailed technical information.

At this point, many people make their decision based on compatibility with existing cross-compilers, debuggers, and other development tools. But it's really up to you to decide what additional features are most important for your project. No matter what you decide to buy, the basic kernel will be about the same as the one described in this chapter. The differences will most likely be measured in processors supported, minimum and maximum memory requirements, availability of add-on software modules (networking protocol stacks, device drivers, and Flash filesystems are common examples), and compatibility with third-party development tools.

Remember that the best reason to choose a commercial operating system is the advantage of using something that is better tested and, therefore, more reliable than a kernel you have developed internally (or obtained for free out of a book). So one of the most important things you should be looking for from your OS vendor is experience. And if your system demands real-time performance, you will definitely want to go with an operating system that has been used successfully in lots of real-time systems. For example, find out which operating system NASA used for its most recent mission. I'd be willing to bet it's a good one.

9

Putting It All Together

In this chapter:
- *Application Overview*
- *Flashing the LED*
- *Printing "Hello, World!"*
- *Working with Serial Ports*
- *The Zilog 85230 Serial Controller*

*A sufficiently high level of technology is
indistinguishable from magic.*
—Arthur C. Clarke

In this chapter, I'll attempt to bring all of the elements we've discussed so far together into a complete embedded application. I don't have much new material to add to the discussion at this point, so the body of the chapter is mainly a description of the code presented herein. My goal is to describe the structure of this application and its source code in such a way that there is no magic remaining for you. You should leave this chapter with a complete understanding of the example program and the ability to develop useful embedded applications of your own.

Application Overview

The application we're going to discuss is not much more complicated than the "Hello, World!" example found in most other programming books. It is a testament to the complexity of embedded software development that this example comes near the end of this book, rather than at its beginning. We've had to gradually build our way up to the computing platform that most books, and even high-level language compilers, take for granted.

Once you're able to write the "Hello, World!" program, your embedded platform starts to look a lot like any other programming environment. The hardest parts of the embedded software development process—familiarizing yourself with the hardware, establishing a software development process for it, and interfacing to the individual hardware devices—are behind you. You are finally able to focus your efforts on the algorithms and user interfaces that are specific to the product you're developing. In many cases, these higher-level aspects of the program can be developed on another computer platform, in parallel with the lower-level embedded software development we've been discussing, and merely ported to the embedded system once both are complete.

Figure 9-1 contains a high-level representation of the "Hello, World!" application. This application includes three device drivers, the ADEOS operating system, and two ADEOS tasks. The first task toggles the Arcom board's red LED at a rate of 10 Hz. The second prints the string "Hello, World!" at 10 second intervals to a host computer or dumb terminal connected to one of the board's serial ports.

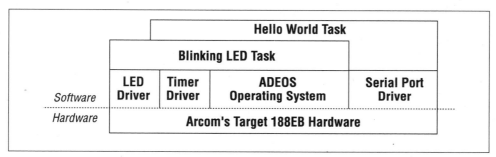

Figure 9-1. The "Hello, World!" application

In addition to the two tasks, there are three device drivers shown in the figure. These control the Arcom board's LEDs, timers, and serial ports, respectively. Although it is customary to draw device drivers below the operating system, I chose to place these three on the same level as the operating system to emphasize that they actually depend more on ADEOS than it does on them. In fact, the embedded operating system doesn't even know (or care) that these drivers are present in the system. This is a common feature of the device drivers and other hardware-specific software in an embedded system.

The implementation of *main* is shown below. This code simply creates the two tasks and starts the operating system's scheduler. At such a high level the code should speak for itself. In fact, we've already discussed a similar code listing in the previous chapter.

```
#include "adeos.h"

void    flashRed(void);
void    helloWorld(void);

/*
 * Create the two tasks.
 */
Task  taskA(flashRed,   150, 512);
Task  taskB(helloWorld, 200, 512);
```

```
/*******************************************************************
 *
 * Function:    main()
 *
 * Description: This function is responsible for starting the ADEOS
 *              scheduler only.
 *
 * Notes:
 *
 * Returns:     This function will never return!
 *
 *******************************************************************/
void
main(void)
{
    os.start();

    // This point will never be reached.

}   /* main() */
```

Flashing the LED

As I said earlier, one of two things this application does is blink the red LED. This is done by the code shown below. Here the function *flashRed* is executed as a task. However, ignoring that and the new function name, this is almost exactly the same Blinking LED function we studied in Chapter 7, *Peripherals*. The only differences at this level are the new frequency (10 Hz) and LED color (red).

```
#include "led.h"
#include "timer.h"


/*******************************************************************
 *
 * Function:    flashRed()
 *
 * Description: Blink the red LED ten times a second.
 *
 * Notes:       This outer loop is hardware-independent.  However, it
 *              calls the hardware-dependent function toggleLed().
 *
 * Returns:     This routine contains an infinite loop.
 *
 *******************************************************************/
void
flashRed(void)
{
    Timer   timer;


    timer.start(50, Periodic);          // Start a periodic 50 ms timer.
```

```
        while (1)
        {
            toggleLed(LED_RED);         // Toggle the red LED.
            timer.waitfor();            // Wait for the timer to expire.
        }

    }   /* flashRed() */
```

The most significant changes to the Blinking LED program are not visible in this code. These are changes made to the *toggleLed* function and the **Timer** class to make them compatible with a multitasking environment. The *toggleLed* function is what I am now calling the LED driver. Once you start thinking about it this way, it might make sense to consider rewriting the driver as a C++ class and add new methods to *set* and *clear* an LED explicitly. However, it is sufficient to leave our implementation as it was in Chapter 7 and simply use a mutex to protect the P2LTCH register from simultaneous access by more than one task.* Here is the modified code:

```
#include "i8018xEB.h"
#include "adeos.h"

static Mutex gLedMutex;

/************************************************************************
 *
 * Function:     toggleLed()
 *
 * Description:  Toggle the state of one or both LEDs.
 *
 * Notes:        This version is ready for multitasking.
 *
 * Returns:      None defined.
 *
 ************************************************************************/
void
toggleLed(unsigned char ledMask)
{
    gLedMutex.take();

    // Read P2LTCH, modify its value, and write the result.
    //
    gProcessor.pPCB->ioPort[1].latch ^= ledMask;
```

* There is a race condition within the earlier *toggleLed* functions. To see it, look back at the code and imagine that two tasks are sharing the LEDs and that the first task has just called that function to toggle the red LED. Inside *toggleLed*, the state of both LEDs is read and stored in a processor register when, all of the sudden, the first task is preempted by the second. Now the second task causes the state of both LEDs to be read once more and stored in another processor register, modified to change the state of the green LED, and the result written out to the P2LTCH register. When the interrupted task is restarted, it already has a copy of the LED state, but this copy is no longer accurate! After making its change to the red LED and writing the new state out to the P2LTCH register, the second task's change will be undone. Adding a mutex eliminates this potential.

```
        gLedMutex.release();

}    /* toggleLed() */
```

A similar change must be made to the timer driver from Chapter 7 before it can be
used in a multitasking environment. However, in this case there is no race condition.* Rather, we need to use a mutex to eliminate the polling in the *waitfor*
method. By associating a mutex with each software timer, we can put any task that
is waiting for a timer to sleep and, thereby, free up the processor for the execution of lower-priority ready tasks. When the awaited timer expires, the sleeping
task will be reawakened by the operating system.

Toward this end, a pointer to a mutex object, called **pMutex**, will be added to the
class definition:

```
class Timer
{
    public:

        Timer();
        ~Timer();

        int    start(unsigned int nMilliseconds, TimerType = OneShot);
        int    waitfor();
        void   cancel();

        TimerState     state;
        TimerType      type;
        unsigned int   length;

        Mutex *        pMutex;

        unsigned int   count;
        Timer *        pNext;

    private:

        static void interrupt  Interrupt();
};
```

This pointer is initialized each time a software timer is created by the constructor.
And, thereafter, whenever a timer object is started, its mutex is taken as follows:

```
/*******************************************************************
 *
 * Method:      start()
 *
 * Description: Start a software timer, based on the tick from the
```

---

* Recall that the timer hardware is initialized only once—during the first constructor invocation—and
thereafter, the timer-specific registers are only read and written by one function: the interrupt service routine.

```
 *                      underlying hardware timer.
 *
 * Notes:        This version is ready for multitasking.
 *
 * Returns:      0 on success, -1 if the timer is already in use.
 *
 ******************************************************************/
int
Timer::start(unsigned int nMilliseconds, TimerType timerType)
{
    if (state != Idle)
    {
        return (-1);
    }

    //
    // Take the mutex.  It will be released when the timer expires.
    //
    pMutex->take();

    //
    // Initialize the software timer.
    //
    state  = Active;
    type   = timerType;
    length = nMilliseconds / MS_PER_TICK;

    //
    // Add this timer to the active timer list.
    //
    timerList.insert(this);

    return (0);

}   /* start() */
```

By taking the mutex when the timer is started, we guarantee that no task (not even the one that started this timer) will be able to take it again until the same mutex is released. And that won't happen until either the timer expires naturally (via the interrupt service routine) or the timer is canceled manually (via the *cancel* method). So the polling loop inside *waitfor* can be replaced with pMutex-> take(), as follows:

```
/******************************************************************
 *
 * Method:       waitfor()
 *
 * Description: Wait for the software timer to finish.
 *
 * Notes:        This version is ready for multitasking.
 *
 * Returns:      0 on success, -1 if the timer is not running.
 *
 ******************************************************************/
```

```
int
Timer::waitfor()
{
    if (state != Active)
    {
        return (-1);
    }

    //
    // Wait for the timer to expire.
    //
    pMutex->take();

    //
    // Restart or idle the timer, depending on its type.
    //
    if (type == Periodic)
    {
        state = Active;
        timerList.insert(this);
    }
    else
    {
        pMutex->release();
        state = Idle;
    }

    return (0);

}   /* waitfor() */
```

When the timer does eventually expire, the interrupt service routine will release the mutex and the calling task will awake inside *waitfor*. In the process of waking, the mutex will already be taken for the next run of the timer. The mutex need only be released if the timer is of type OneShot and, because of that, not automatically restarted.

Printing "Hello, World!"

The other part of our example application is a task that prints the text string "Hello, World!" to one of the serial ports at a regular interval. Again, the timer driver is used to create the periodicity. However, this task also depends on a serial port driver that we haven't seen before. The guts of the serial driver will be described in the final two sections of this chapter, but the task that uses it is shown here. The only thing you need to know about serial ports to understand this task is that a SerialPort is a C++ class and that the *puts* method is used to print a string of characters from that port.

```
#include "timer.h"
#include "serial.h"
```

```
/********************************************************************
 *
 * Function:     helloWorld()
 *
 * Description:  Send a text message to the serial port periodically.
 *
 * Notes:        This outer loop is hardware-independent.
 *
 * Returns:      This routine contains an infinite loop.
 *
 ********************************************************************/
void
helloWorld(void)
{
    Timer         timer;
    SerialPort    serial(PORTA, 19200L);


    timer.start(10000, Periodic);       // Start a periodic 10 s timer.

    while (1)
    {
        serial.puts("Hello, World!");   // Output a simple text message.
        timer.waitfor();                // Wait for the timer to expire.
    }

}   /* helloWorld() */
```

Though the periodicity has a different length, the general structure of this task is the same as that of the *flashRed* function. So, the only thing left for us to discuss is the makeup of the serial port driver. We'll start with a description of a generalized serial ports interface and then finish with the specifics of the serial controller found on the Arcom board.

Working with Serial Ports

At the application level, a serial port is simply a bidirectional data channel. This channel is usually terminated on each end with a hardware device called a serial communications controller (SCC). Each serial port within the SCC—there are usually at least two serial ports per controller—is connected to the embedded processor on one side and to a cable (or the connector for one) on the other side. At the other end of that cable there is usually a host computer (or some other embedded system) that has an internal serial communications controller of its own.

Of course, the actual purpose of the serial port is application-dependent. But the general idea is this: to communicate streams of data between two intelligent systems or between one such device (the target) and a human operator. Typically, the smallest unit of data that can be sent or received over a serial port is an 8-bit character. So streams of binary data need to be reorganized into bytes before transmission. This restriction is similar to that of C's *stdio* library, so it makes sense to borrow some programming conventions from that interface.

In order to support serial communications and emulate a *stdio*-style interface, I've defined the `SerialPort` class as it is shown below. This class abstracts the application's use of the serial port as bidirectional data channel and makes the interface as similar as possible to what we've all seen before. In addition to the constructor and destructor, the class includes four methods—*putchar,** puts, getchar,* and *gets*— for sending characters and strings of characters and receiving the same. These routines are defined exactly as they would be in any ANSI C–compliant version of the header file *stdio.h*.

Here's the actual class definition:

```
#include "circbuf.h"

#define PORTA  0
#define PORTB  1

class SerialPort
{
    public:

        SerialPort(int           port,
                   unsigned long  baudRate = 19200L,
                   unsigned int   txQueueSize = 64,    // Transmit Buffer Size
                   unsigned int   rxQueueSize = 64);   // Receive Buffer Size
        ~SerialPort();

        int       putchar(int c);
        int       puts(const char *s);

        int       getchar();
        char *    gets(char *s);

    private:

        int       channel;

        CircBuf *  pTxQueue;                 // Transmit Buffer
        CircBuf *  pRxQueue;                 // Receive Buffer
};
```

Note the private data members **channel**, **pTxQueue**, and **pRxQueue**. These are initialized within the constructor and used to interface to the hardware-specific part of the serial driver described in the next section. I'll have more to say about this interface shortly, but for now just be aware that the **SerialPort** class does not

---

* You might be wondering why this method accepts an integer argument rather than a character. After all, we're sending 8-bit characters over the serial port, right? Well, don't ask me. I'm just trying to be consistent with the ANSI C library standard and wondering the very same thing myself.

contain any code that is specific to a particular Serial Controller. All of that is hidden inside the SCC class that it references.

Let's take a look at the *SerialPort* constructor. This routine is responsible for initializing the three private data members and configuring the requested data channel within the SCC hardware:

```cpp
#include "scc.h"

static SCC  scc;

/***********************************************************************
 *
 * Method:       SerialPort()
 *
 * Description: Default constructor for the serial port class.
 *
 * Notes:
 *
 * Returns:      None defined.
 *
 ***********************************************************************/
SerialPort::SerialPort(int             port,
                       unsigned long  baudRate,
                       unsigned int   txQueueSize,
                       unsigned int   rxQueueSize)
{
    //
    // Initialize the logical device.
    //
    switch (port)
    {
      case PORTA:
        channel = 0;
        break;

      case PORTB:
        channel = 1;
        break;

      default:
        channel = -1;
        break;
    }

    //
    // Create input and output FIFOs.
    //
    pTxQueue = new CircBuf(txQueueSize);
    pRxQueue = new CircBuf(rxQueueSize);

    //
    // Initialize the hardware device.
```

```
        //
        scc.reset(channel);
        scc.init(channel, baudRate, pTxQueue, pRxQueue);

}    /* SerialPort() */
```

Once a `SerialPort` object has been created, the aforementioned methods for sending and receiving data can be used. For example, in the *helloWorld* function shown earlier, `puts("Hello, World!")` is the statement that sends the text string to serial port A (a.k.a. SCC channel 0). The data is sent over the serial channel at a rate of 19,200 bits per second, as selected by the `baudRate` parameter to the *SerialPort* constructor.

The send and receive methods rely on the circular buffers pointed to by `pTxQueue` and `pRxQueue`, respectively. `pTxQueue` is a transmit buffer that provides overflow memory in case the rate at which characters are sent by the application exceeds the baud rate of the channel. This usually happens in short spurts, so it is expected that the transmit buffer won't usually fill up all the way. Similarly, the receive buffer, `pRxQueue`, provides overflow memory for bytes that have been received at the serial port but not yet read by the application. By default, the above constructor creates each of these as 64-byte buffers. However, these sizes can be set to smaller or larger values, depending on the needs of your application, simply by overriding the default arguments to the constructor.

The implementations of the send methods *putchar* and *puts* are shown below. In *putchar* we start by checking if the transmit buffer is already full. If so, we return an error indication to the caller, so he will know that the character was not sent. Otherwise, we add the new character to the transmit buffer, ensure that the SCC transmit engine is running, and return success. The *puts* method makes a series of calls to *putchar*, one for each character in the string and then adds a newline character at the end.

```
/*********************************************************************
 *
 * Method:      putchar()
 *
 * Description: Write one character to the serial port.
 *
 * Notes:
 *
 * Returns:     The transmitted character is returned on success.
 *              -1 is returned in the case of an error.
 *
 *********************************************************************/
int
SerialPort::putchar(int c)
{
    if (pTxQueue->isFull())
    {
```

```
        return (-1);
    }

    //
    // Add the character to the transmit FIFO.
    //
    pTxQueue->add((char) c);

    //
    // Start the transmit engine (if it's stalled).
    //
    scc.txStart(channel);

    return (c);

}   /* putchar() */


/*********************************************************************
 *
 * Method:      puts()
 *
 * Description: Copies the null-terminated string s to the serial
 *              port and appends a newline character.
 *
 * Notes:       In rare cases, this function may return success though
 *              the newline was not actually sent.
 *
 * Returns:     The number of characters transmitted successfully.
 *              Otherwise, -1 is returned to indicate error.
 *
 *********************************************************************/
int
SerialPort::puts(const char * s)
{
    const char *  p;


    //
    // Send each character of the string.
    //
    for (p = s; *p != '\0'; p++)
    {
        if (putchar(*p) < 0) break;
    }

    //
    // Add a newline character.
    //
    putchar('\n');

    return ((p - s) + 1);

}   /* puts() */
```

The receive method *getchar* is similar to *putchar*. It starts by checking if the receive buffer is empty. If so, an error code is returned. Otherwise, one byte of data is removed from the receive buffer and returned to the caller. The *gets* method calls *getchar* repeatedly until either a newline character is found or there is no more data available at the serial port. It then returns whatever string was found up to that point. The code for both of these methods follows:

```
/*********************************************************************
 *
 * Method:       getchar()
 *
 * Description: Read one character from the serial port.
 *
 * Notes:
 *
 * Returns:      The next character found on this input stream.
 *               -1 is returned in the case of an error.
 *
 *********************************************************************/
int
SerialPort::getchar(void)
{
    int  c;


    if (pRxQueue->isEmpty())
    {
        return (-1);                    // There is no input data available.
    }

    int rxStalled = pRxQueue->isFull();

    //
    // Read the next byte out of the receive FIFO.
    //
    c = pRxQueue->remove();

    //
    // If the receive engine is stalled, restart it.
    //
    if (rxStalled)
    {
        scc.rxStart(channel);
    }

    return (c);

}   /* getchar() */
```

```
/*********************************************************************
 *
 * Method:       gets()
 *
 * Description:  Collects a string of characters terminated by a new-
 *               line character from the serial port and places it in s.
 *               The newline character is replaced by a null character.
 *
 * Notes:        The caller is responsible for allocating adequate space
 *               for the string.
 *
 * Warnings:     This function does not block waiting for a newline.
 *               If a complete string is not found, it will return
 *               whatever is available in the receive queue.
 *
 * Returns:      A pointer to the string.
 *               Otherwise, NULL is returned to indicate an error.
 *
 *********************************************************************/
char *
SerialPort::gets(char * s)
{
    char *  p;
    int     c;


    //
    // Read characters until a newline is found or no more data.
    //
    for (p = s; (c = getchar()) != '\n' && c >= 0; p++)
    {
        *p = c;
    }

    //
    // Terminate the string.
    //
    *p = '\0';

    return (s);

}   /* gets() */
```

The Zilog 85230 Serial Controller

The two serial ports on the Arcom board are part of the same Zilog 85230 Serial Communications Controller. This particular chip is, unfortunately, rather compli-cated to configure and use. So, rather than fill up the `SerialPort` class shown earlier with device-specific code, I decided to divide the serial driver into two parts. The upper layer is the class we have just discussed. This upper layer will work with any two-channel SCC that provides byte-oriented transmit and receive interfaces and configurable baud rates. All that is necessary is to implement a device-specific SCC class (the lower layer described next) that has the same *reset*, *init*, *txStart*, and *rxStart* interfaces as those called from the `SerialPort` class.

In fact, one of the reasons the Zilog 85230 SCC device is so difficult to configure and use is that it has many more options than are really necessary for this simple application. The chip is capable of sending not only bytes but also characters that have any number of bits up to 8. And in addition to being able to select the baud rate, it is also possible to configure many other features of one or both channels and to support a variety of other communication protocols.

Here's how the SCC class is actually defined:

```
#include "circbuf.h"

class SCC
{
    public:

        SCC();

        void   reset(int channel);
        void   init(int channel, unsigned long baudRate,
                    CircBuf * pTxQueue, CircBuf * pRxQueue);

        void   txStart(int channel);
        void   rxStart(int channel);

    private:

        static void interrupt  Interrupt(void);
};
```

Notice that this class also depends upon the `CircBuf` class. The **pTxQueue** and **pRxQueue** arguments to the *init* method are used to establish the input and output buffers for that channel. This makes it possible to link a logical `SerialPort` object with one of the physical channels within the SCC device. The reason for defining the *init* method separately from the constructor is that most SCC chips control two or more serial channels. The constructor resets them both the first time it is called. Then, *init* is called to set the baud rate and other parameters for a particular channel.

Everything else about the SCC class is an internal feature that is specific to the Zilog 85230 device. For that reason, I have decided not to list or explain this rather long and complex module within the book. Suffice it to say that the code consists of macros for reading and writing the registers of the device, an interrupt service routine to handle receive and transmit interrupts, and methods for restarting the receive and transmit processes if they have previously stalled while waiting for more data. Interested readers will find the actual code in the file *scc.cpp*.

In this chapter:
- *Increasing Code Efficiency*
- *Decreasing Code Size*
- *Reducing Memory Usage*
- *Limiting the Impact of C++*

10

Optimizing Your Code

> *Things should be made as simple as possible,*
> *but not any simpler.*
> —Albert Einstein

Though getting the software to work correctly seems like the logical last step for a project, this is not always the case in embedded systems development. The need for low-cost versions of our products drives hardware designers to provide just barely enough memory and processing power to get the job done. Of course, during the software development phase of the project it is more important to get the program to work correctly. And toward that end there are usually one or more "development" boards around, each with additional memory, a faster processor, or both. These boards are used to get the software working correctly, and then the final phase of the project becomes code optimization. The goal of this final step is to make the working program run on the lower-cost "production" version of the hardware.

Increasing Code Efficiency

Some degree of code optimization is provided by all modern C and C++ compilers. However, most of the optimization techniques that are performed by a compiler involve a tradeoff between execution speed and code size. Your program can be made either faster or smaller, but not both. In fact, an improvement in one of these areas can have a negative impact on the other. It is up to the programmer to decide which of these improvements is most important to her. Given that single piece of information, the compiler's optimization phase can make the appropriate choice whenever a speed versus size tradeoff is encountered.

Because you can't have the compiler perform both types of optimization for you, I recommend letting it do what it can to reduce the size of your program. Execution speed is usually important only within certain time-critical or frequently executed sections of the code, and there are many things you can do to improve the efficiency of those sections by hand. However, code size is a difficult thing to influence manually, and the compiler is in a much better position to make this change across all of your software modules.

By the time your program is working you might already know, or have a pretty good idea, which subroutines and modules are the most critical for overall code efficiency. Interrupt service routines, high-priority tasks, calculations with real-time deadlines, and functions that are either compute-intensive or frequently called are all likely candidates. A tool called a *profiler*, included with some software development suites, can be used to narrow your focus to those routines in which the program spends most (or too much) of its time.

Once you've identified the routines that require greater code efficiency, one or more of the following techniques can be used to reduce their execution time:

Inline functions

In C++, the keyword `inline` can be added to any function declaration. This keyword makes a request to the compiler to replace all calls to the indicated function with copies of the code that is inside. This eliminates the runtime overhead associated with the actual function call and is most effective when the inline function is called frequently but contains only a few lines of code.

Inline functions provide a perfect example of how execution speed and code size are sometimes inversely linked. The repetitive addition of the inline code will increase the size of your program in direct proportion to the number of times the function is called. And, obviously, the larger the function, the more significant the size increase will be. The resulting program runs faster, but now requires more ROM.

Table lookups

A `switch` statement is one common programming technique to be used with care. Each test and jump that makes up the machine language implementation uses up valuable processor time simply deciding what work should be done next. To speed things up, try to put the individual cases in order by their relative frequency of occurrence. In other words, put the most likely cases first and the least likely cases last. This will reduce the average execution time, though it will not improve at all upon the worst-case time.

If there is a lot of work to be done within each case, it might be more efficient to replace the entire `switch` statement with a table of pointers to functions. For example, the following block of code is a candidate for this improvement:

```
enum NodeType { NodeA, NodeB, NodeC };

switch (getNodeType())
{
    case NodeA:
        .
        .
        .
    case NodeB:
        .
        .
        .
    case NodeC:
        .
        .
        .
}
```

To speed things up, we would replace this **switch** statement with the following alternative. The first part of this is the setup: the creation of an array of function pointers. The second part is a one-line replacement for the **switch** statement that executes more efficiently.

```
int processNodeA(void);
int processNodeB(void);
int processNodeC(void);

/*
 * Establishment of a table of pointers to functions.
 */
int (*func)() nodeFunctions[] = { processNodeA, processNodeB, processNodeC };

    .
    .

/*
 * The entire switch statement is replaced by the next line.
 */
status = nodeFunctions[getNodeType()]();
```

Hand-coded assembly

Some software modules are best written in assembly language. This gives the programmer an opportunity to make them as efficient as possible. Though most C/C++ compilers produce much better machine code than the average programmer, a good programmer can still do better than the average compiler for a given function. For example, early in my career I implemented a digital filtering algorithm in C and targeted it to a TI TMS320C30 DSP. The compiler we had back then was either unaware or unable to take advantage of a special instruction that performed exactly the mathematical operations I needed. By manually replacing one loop of the C program with inline assembly instructions that did the same thing, I was able to decrease the overall computation time by more than a factor of ten.

Register variables

The keyword **register** can be used when declaring local variables. This asks the compiler to place the variable into a general-purpose register, rather than on the stack. Used judiciously, this technique provides hints to the compiler about the most frequently accessed variables and will somewhat enhance the performance of the function. The more frequently the function is called, the more likely such a change is to improve the code's performance.

Global variables

It is more efficient to use a global variable than to pass a parameter to a function. This eliminates the need to push the parameter onto the stack before the function call and pop it back off once the function is completed. In fact, the most efficient implementation of any subroutine would have no parameters at all. However, the decision to use a global variable can also have some negative effects on the program. The software engineering community generally discourages the use of global variables, in an effort to promote the goals of modularity and reentrancy, which are also important considerations.

Polling

Interrupt service routines are often used to improve program efficiency. However, there are some rare cases in which the overhead associated with the interrupts actually causes an inefficiency. These are cases in which the average time between interrupts is of the same order of magnitude as the interrupt latency. In such cases it might be better to use polling to communicate with the hardware device. Of course, this too leads to a less modular software design.

Fixed-point arithmetic

Unless your target platform includes a floating-point coprocessor, you'll pay a very large penalty for manipulating **float** data in your program. The compiler-supplied floating-point library contains a set of software subroutines that emulate the instruction set of a floating-point coprocessor. Many of these functions take a long time to execute relative to their integer counterparts and also might not be reentrant.

· If you are only using floating-point for a few calculations, it might be better to reimplement the calculations themselves using fixed-point arithmetic only. Although it might be difficult to see just how this can be done, it is theoretically possible to perform any floating-point calculation with fixed-point arithmetic. (After all, that's how the floating-point software library does it, right?) Your biggest advantage is that you probably don't need to implement the entire IEEE 754 standard just to perform one or two calculations. If you do need that kind of complete functionality, stick with the compiler's floating-point library and look for other ways to speed up your program.

Decreasing Code Size

As I said earlier, when it comes to reducing code size your best bet is to let the compiler do the work for you. However, if the resulting program is still too large for your available ROM, there are several programming techniques you can use to further reduce the size of your program. In this section we'll discuss both automatic and manual code size optimizations.

Of course, Murphy's Law dictates that the first time you enable the compiler's optimization feature your previously working program will suddenly fail. Perhaps the most notorious of the automatic optimizations is "dead code elimination." This optimization eliminates code that the compiler believes to be either redundant or irrelevant. For example, adding zero to a variable requires no runtime calculation whatsoever. But you might still want the compiler to generate those "irrelevant" instructions if they perform some function that the compiler doesn't know about.

For example, given the following block of code, most optimizing compilers would remove the first statement because the value of ***pControl** is not used before it is overwritten (on the third line):

```
*pControl = DISABLE;
*pData    = 'a';
*pControl = ENABLE;
```

But what if **pControl** and **pData** are actually pointers to memory-mapped device registers? In that case, the peripheral device would not receive the **DISABLE** command before the byte of data was written. This could potentially wreak havoc on all future interactions between the processor and this peripheral. To protect yourself from such problems, you must declare all pointers to memory-mapped registers and global variables that are shared between threads (or a thread and an ISR) with the keyword **volatile**. And if you miss just one of them, Murphy's Law will come back to haunt you in the final days of your project. I guarantee it.

Never make the mistake of assuming that the optimized program will behave the same as the unoptimized one. You must completely retest your software at each new optimization level to be sure its behavior hasn't changed.

To make matters worse, debugging an optimized program is challenging, to say the least. With the compiler's optimization enabled, the correlation between a line of source code and the set of processor instructions that implements that line is much weaker. Those particular instructions might have moved or been split up, or two similar code blocks might now share a common implementation. In fact, some lines of the high-level language program might have been removed from the program altogether (as they were in the previous example)! As a result, you might be unable to set a breakpoint on a particular line of the program or examine the value of a variable of interest.

Once you've got the automatic optimizations working, here are some tips for further reducing the size of your code by hand:

Avoid standard library routines

One of the best things you can do to reduce the size of your program is to avoid using large standard library routines. Many of the largest are expensive only because they try to handle all possible cases. It might be possible to implement a subset of the functionality yourself with significantly less code. For example, the standard C library's *sprintf* routine is notoriously large. Much of this bulk is located within the floating-point manipulation routines on which it depends. But if you don't need to format and display floating-point values (%f or %d), you could write your own integer-only version of *sprintf* and save several kilobytes of code space. In fact, a few implementations of the standard C library (Cygnus' *newlib* comes to mind) include just such a function, called *siprintf*.

Native word size

Every processor has a native word size, and the ANSI C and C++ standards state that data type int must always map to that size. Manipulation of smaller and larger data types sometimes requires the use of additional machine-language instructions. By consistently using int whenever possible in your program, you might be able to shave a precious few hundred bytes from your program.

Goto statements

As with global variables, good software engineering practice dictates against the use of this technique. But in a pinch, goto statements can be used to remove complicated control structures or to share a block of oft repeated code.

In addition to these techniques, several of the ones described in the previous section could be helpful, specifically table lookups, hand-coded assembly, register variables, and global variables. Of these, the use of hand-coded assembly will usually yield the largest decrease in code size.

Reducing Memory Usage

In some cases, it is RAM rather than ROM that is the limiting factor for your application. In these cases, you'll want to reduce your dependence on global data, the stack, and the heap. These are all optimizations better made by the programmer than by the compiler.

Because ROM is usually cheaper than RAM (on a per-byte basis), one acceptable strategy for reducing the amount of global data might be to move constant data into ROM. This can be done automatically by the compiler if you declare all of your constant data with the keyword const. Most C/C++ compilers place all of the constant global data they encounter into a special data segment that is recognizable to the locator as ROM-able. This technique is most valuable if there are lots of strings or table-oriented data that does not change at runtime.

If some of the data is fixed once the program is running but not necessarily constant, the constant data segment could be placed in a hybrid memory device instead. This memory device could then be updated over a network or by a technician assigned to make the change. An example of such data is the sales tax rate for each locale in which your product will be deployed. If a tax rate changes, the memory device can be updated, but additional RAM can be saved in the meantime.

Stack size reductions can also lower your program's RAM requirement. One way to figure out exactly how much stack you need is to fill the entire memory area reserved for the stack with a special data pattern. Then, after the software has been running for a while—preferably under both normal and stressful conditions—use a debugger to examine the modified stack. The part of the stack memory area that still contains your special data pattern has never been overwritten, so it is safe to reduce the size of the stack area by that amount.[*]

Be especially conscious of stack space if you are using a real-time operating system. Most operating systems create a separate stack for each task. These stacks are used for function calls and interrupt service routines that occur within the context of a task. You can determine the amount of stack required for each task stack in the manner described earlier. You might also try to reduce the number of tasks or switch to an operating system that has a separate "interrupt stack" for execution of all interrupt service routines. The latter method can significantly reduce the stack size requirement of each task.

The size of the heap is limited to the amount of RAM left over after all of the global data and stack space has been allocated. If the heap is too small, your program will not be able to allocate memory when it is needed, so always be sure to compare the result of *malloc* or new with NULL before dereferencing it. If you've tried all of these suggestions and your program is still requiring too much memory, you might have no choice but to eliminate the heap altogether.

---

[*] Of course, you might want to leave a little extra space on the stack—just in case your testing didn't last long enough or did not accurately reflect all possible runtime scenarios. Never forget that a stack overflow is a potentially fatal event for your software and to be avoided at all costs.

Limiting the Impact of C++

One of the biggest issues I faced upon deciding to write this book was whether or not to include C++ in the discussion. Despite my familiarity with C++, I had written almost all of my embedded software in C and assembly. In addition, there has been much debate within the embedded software community about whether C++ is worth the performance penalty. It is generally agreed that C++ programs produce larger executables that run more slowly than programs written entirely in C. However, C++ has many benefits for the programmer, and I wanted to talk about some of those benefits in the book. So I ultimately decided to include C++ in the discussion, but to use in my examples only those features with the least performance penalty.

I believe that many readers will face the same issue in their own embedded systems programming. Before ending the book, I wanted to briefly justify each of the C++ features I have used and to warn you about some of the more expensive features that I did not use.

Of course, not everything introduced in C++ is expensive. Many older C++ compilers incorporate a technology called C-front that turns C++ programs into C and feeds the result into a standard C compiler. The mere fact that this is possible should suggest that the syntactical differences between the languages have little or no runtime cost associated with them.* It is only the newest C++ features, like templates, that cannot be handled in this manner.

For example, the definition of a **class** is completely benign. The list of public and private member data and functions are not much different than a **struct** and a list of function prototypes. However, the C++ compiler is able to use the **public** and **private** keywords to determine which method calls and data accesses are allowed and disallowed. Because this determination is made at compile time, there is no penalty paid at runtime. The addition of classes alone does not affect either the code size or efficiency of your programs.

Default parameter values are also penalty-free. The compiler simply inserts code to pass the default value whenever the function is called without an argument in that position. Similarly, function name overloading is a compile-time modification. Functions with the same names but different parameters are each assigned unique names during the compilation process. The compiler alters the function name each time it appears in your program, and the linker matches them up appropriately. I haven't used this feature of C++ in any of my examples, but I could have done so without affecting performance.

---

* Moreover, it should be clear that there is no penalty for compiling an ordinary C program with a C++ compiler.

The Embedded C++ Standard

You might be wondering why the creators of the C++ language included so many expensive—in terms of execution time and code size—features. You are not alone; people around the world have wondered the same thing—especially the users of C++ for embedded programming. Many of these expensive features are recent additions that are neither strictly necessary nor part of the original C++ specification. These features have been added one by one as part of the ongoing "standardization" process.

In 1996, a group of Japanese processor vendors joined together to define a subset of the C++ language and libraries that is better suited for embedded software development. They call their new industry standard Embedded C++. Surprisingly, for its young age, it has already generated a great deal of interest and excitement within the C++ user community.

A proper subset of the draft C++ standard, Embedded C++ omits pretty much anything that can be left out without limiting the expressiveness of the underlying language. This includes not only expensive features like multiple inheritance, virtual base classes, runtime type identification, and exception handling, but also some of the newest additions like templates, namespaces, and new-style casts. What's left is a simpler version of C++ that is still object-oriented and a superset of C, but with significantly less runtime overhead and smaller runtime libraries.

A number of commercial C++ compilers already support the Embedded C++ standard specifically. Several others allow you to manually disable individual language features, thus enabling you to emulate Embedded C++ or create your very own flavor of the C++ language.

Operator overloading is another feature I could have used but didn't. Whenever the compiler sees such an operator, it simply replaces it with the appropriate function call. So in the code listing that follows, the last two lines are equivalent and the performance penalty is easily understood:

```
Complex  a, b, c;

c = operator+(a, b);            // The traditional way: Function Call
c = a + b;                      // The C++ way: Operator Overloading
```

Constructors and destructors also have a slight penalty associated with them. These special methods are guaranteed to be called each time an object of the type is created or goes out of scope, respectively. However, this small amount of overhead is a reasonable price to pay for fewer bugs. Constructors eliminate an entire class of C programming errors having to do with uninitialized data structures. This feature has also proved useful for hiding the awkward initialization sequences that are associated with complex classes like `Timer` and `Task`.

Virtual functions also have a reasonable cost/benefit ratio. Without going into too much detail about what virtual functions are, let's just say that polymorphism would be impossible without them. And without polymorphism, C++ would not be a true object-oriented language. The only significant cost of virtual functions is one additional memory lookup before a virtual function can be called. Ordinary function and method calls are not affected.

The features of C++ that are too expensive for my taste are templates, exceptions, and runtime type identification. All three of these negatively impact code size, and exceptions and runtime type identification also increase execution time. Before deciding whether to use these features, you might want to do some experiments to see how they will affect the size and speed of your own application.

Appendix:
Arcom's Target188EB

All of the examples in this book have been written for and tested on an embedded platform called the Target188EB. This board is a low-cost, high-speed embedded controller designed, manufactured, and sold by Arcom Control Systems. The following paragraphs contain information about the hardware, required and included software development tools, and instructions for ordering a board for yourself.

The Target188EB hardware consists of the following:

- Processor: Intel 80188EB (25 MHz)
- RAM: 128K of SRAM (256K available), with optional battery backup
- ROM: 128K of EPROM and 128K of Flash (512K maximum)
- Two RS232-compatible serial ports (with external DB9 connectors)
- 24-channel parallel port
- 3 programmable timer/counters
- 4 available interrupt inputs
- An 8-bit PC/104 expansion bus interface
- An optional 8-bit STEBus expansion interface
- A remote debugging adapter containing two additional RS232-compatible serial ports

Software development for this board is as easy as PC programming. Free development tools and utilities included with the board allow you to develop your embedded application in C/C++ or assembly language, using Borland's C++ compiler and Turbo Assembler. In addition, a debug monitor preinstalled in the onboard Flash memory makes it possible to use Borland's Turbo Debugger to easily find and fix bugs in your application. Finally, a library of hardware interface routines makes manipulating the onboard hardware as simple as interacting with C's *stdio* library.

All of the programs in this book were assembled, compiled, linked, and debugged with a copy of Borland C++ 3.1. However, any version of the Borland tool chain capable of producing code for an 80186 processor will do just fine. This includes the popular versions 3.1, 4.5, and 4.52. If you already have one of these versions, you can use that. Otherwise, you might want to check with Arcom to find out if the latest version of Borland's tools is compatible with their development and debugging tools.

In small quantities, the Target188EB board (part number TARGET188EB-SBC) retails for $195.* Ordinarily, this does not include the software development tools and power supply. However, Arcom has generously agreed to provide a free copy of their Target Development Kit (a $100 value) to readers of this book.† Simply mention the book when placing your order and you will be eligible for this special offer. To place an order, contact the manufacturer directly at:

> Arcom Control Systems
> 13510 South Oak Street
> Kansas City, MO 64145
> Phone: 888-941-2224
> Fax: 816-941-7807
> Email: *sales@arcomcontrols.com*
> Web: *http://www.arcomcontrols.com/*

---

* The price and availability of this board are beyond my control. Please contact Arcom for the latest information.

† No financial or contractual relationship exists between myself or O'Reilly & Associates, Inc. and Arcom Control Systems. I only promote the board here out of thanks to Arcom for producing a quality product and supporting me with this project.

Glossary

ASIC

Application-Specific Integrated Circuit. A piece of custom-designed hardware in a chip.

address bus

A set of electrical lines connected to the *processor* and all of the *peripherals* with which it communicates. The address bus is used by the processor to select a specific memory location or *register* within a particular peripheral. If the address bus contains n electrical lines, the processor can uniquely address up to 2^n such locations.

application software

Software modules specific to a particular embedded project. The application software is unlikely to be reusable across embedded platforms, simply because each *embedded system* has a different application.

assembler

A software development tool that translates human-readable *assembly language* programs into machine-language instructions that the *processor* can understand and execute.

assembly language

A human-readable form of a *processor's* instruction set. Most *processor-specific* functions must be written in assembly language.

binary semaphore

A type of *semaphore* that has only two states. Also called a *mutex*.

board support package

Part of a software package that is *processor*- or platform-dependent. Typically, sample source code for the board support package is provided by the package developer. The sample code must be modified as necessary, compiled, and linked with the rest of the software package.

breakpoint

A location in a program at which execution is to be stopped and control of the processor switched to the *debugger*. Mechanisms for creating and removing breakpoints are provided by most debugging tools.

CISC

Complex Instruction Set Computer. Describes the architecture of a *processor family*. CISC processors generally feature variable-length instructions and multiple addressing formats, and contain only a small number of general-purpose *registers*. Intel's 80x86 family is the quintessential example of CISC. Contrast with *RISC*.

CPU

Central Processing Unit. The part of a *processor* that executes instructions.

compiler

A software development tool that translates *high-level language* programs into the machine-language instructions that a particular *processor* can understand and execute.

context

The current state of the *registers* and flags of the *processor*.

context switch

The process of switching from one *task* to another in a *multitasking* operating system. A context switch involves saving the *context* of the running task and restoring the previously saved context of the other. The piece of code that does this is necessarily *processor-specific*.

counting semaphore

A type of *semaphore* that is used to track multiple resources of the same type. An attempt to take a counting semaphore is blocked only if all of the available resources are in use. Contrast with *binary semaphore*.

critical section

A block of code that must be executed in sequence and without interruption to guarantee correct operation of the software. See also *race condition*.

cross-compiler

A *compiler* that runs on a different platform than the one for which it produces *object code*. A cross-compiler runs on a *host* computer and produces object code for the *target*.

DMA

Direct Memory Access. A technique for transferring data directly between two *peripherals* (usually memory and an I/O device) with only minimal intervention by the *processor*. DMA transfers are managed by a third *peripheral* called a DMA controller.

DRAM

Dynamic Random-Access Memory. A type of RAM that maintains its contents only as long as the data stored in the device is refreshed at regular intervals. The refresh cycles are usually performed by a *peripheral* called a DRAM controller.

DSP

See *digital signal processor*.

data bus

A set of electrical lines connected to the *processor* and all of the *peripherals* with which it communicates. When the processor wants to read (or write) the contents of a memory location or *register* within a particular peripheral, it sets the *address bus* pins appropriately and receives (or transmits) the contents on the data bus.

deadline

The time by which a particular set of computations must be completed. See also *real-time system*.

deadlock

An unwanted software situation in which an entire set of tasks is blocked, waiting for an event that only a task within the same set can cause. If a deadlock occurs, the only solution is to reset the system. However, it is usually possible to prevent deadlocks altogether by following certain software design practices.

debug monitor

A piece of embedded software that has been designed specifically for use as a debugging tool. It usually resides in *ROM* and communicates with a *debugger* via a serial port or network connection. The debug monitor provides a set of primitive commands to view and modify memory locations and *registers*, create and remove *breakpoints*, and execute your program. The debugger combines these primitives to fulfill higher-level requests like program download and single-step.

debugger

A software development tool used to test and debug embedded software. The debugger runs on a *host* computer and connects to the *target* through a serial port or network connection. Using a debugger, you can download software to the target for immediate execution. You can also set *breakpoints* and examine the contents of specific memory locations and *registers*.

device driver

A software module that hides the details of a particular *peripheral* and provides a high-level programming interface to it.

device programmer

A tool for programming nonvolatile memories and other electrically program-mable devices. Typically, the programmable device is inserted into a socket on the device programmer and the contents of a memory buffer are then trans-ferred into it.

digital signal processor

A device that is similar to a *microprocessor,* except that the internal CPU has been optimized for use in applications involving discrete-time signal process-ing. In addition to standard microprocessor instructions, DSPs usually support a set of complex instructions to perform common signal-processing computations quickly. Common DSP families are TI's 320Cxx and Motorola's 5600x series.

EEPROM

Electrically Erasable, Programmable Read-Only Memory. (Pronounced "dou-ble-E PROM.") A type of *PROM* that can be erased electronically.

EPROM

Erasable, Programmable Read-Only Memory. A type of *PROM* that can be erased by exposing it to ultraviolet light. Once erased, an EPROM can be reprogrammed with the help of a *device programmer.*

embedded system

A combination of computer hardware and software, and perhaps additional mechanical or other parts, designed to perform a specific function. Contrast with *general-purpose computer.*

emulator

Short for In-Circuit Emulator (ICE). A debugging tool that takes the place of—emulates—the *processor* on your *target* board. Emulators frequently incorpo-rate a special "bond-out" version of the target processor that allows you to observe and record its internal state as your program is executing.

executable

A file containing *object code* that is ready for execution on the *target.* All that remains is to place the object code into a *ROM* or download it via a debug-ging tool.

firmware

Embedded software that is stored as *object code* within a ROM. This name is most common among the programmers of *digital signal processors.*

Flash memory

A *RAM-ROM* hybrid that can be erased and rewritten under software control. Such devices are divided into blocks, called sectors, that are individually eras-able. Flash memory is common in systems that require nonvolatile data storage at very low cost. In some cases, a large Flash memory is even used instead of a disk-drive.

general-purpose computer

A combination of computer hardware and software that serves as a general-purpose computing platform. For example, a personal computer. Contrast with *embedded system*.

HLL

See *high-level language*.

heap

An area of memory that is used for dynamic memory allocation. Calls to *malloc* and *free* and the C++ operators **new** and **delete** result in runtime manipulation of the heap.

high-level language

A language, such as C or C++, that is *processor-independent*. When you program in a high-level language, it is possible to concentrate on algorithms and applications without wórrying about the details of a particular *processor*.

host

A *general-purpose computer* that communicates with the *target* via a serial port or network connection. This term is usually used to distinguish the computer on which the *debugger* is running from the *embedded system* that is being developed.

ICE

In-Circuit Emulator. See *emulator*.

I/O

Input/Output. The interface between a *processor* and the world around it. The simplest examples are switches (inputs) and LEDs (outputs).

I/O device

A piece of hardware that interfaces between the *processor* and the outside world. Common examples are switches and LEDs, serial ports, and network controllers.

I/O map

A table or diagram containing the name and address range of each *peripheral* addressable by the *processor* within the *I/O space*. I/O maps are a helpful aid in getting to know the hardware.

I/O space

A special memory region provided by some *processors* and generally reserved for the attachment of *I/O devices*. Memory locations and *registers* within an I/O space can be accessed only via special instructions. For example, processors in the 80x86 family have special I/O space instructions called **in** and **out**. Contrast with *memory space*.

ISR

See *interrupt service routine*.

instruction pointer

A *register* in the *processor* that contains the address of the next instruction to be executed. Also known as a *program counter.*

interrupt

An asynchronous electrical signal from a *peripheral* to the *processor.* When the peripheral asserts this signal, we say that an interrupt occurs. When an interrupt occurs, the current state of the processor is saved and an *interrupt service routine* is executed. When the interrupt service routine exits, control of the processor is returned to whatever part of the software was previously running.

interrupt latency

The amount of time between the assertion of an *interrupt* and the start of the associated *interrupt service routine.*

interrupt service routine

A piece of software executed in response to a particular *interrupt.*

interrupt type

A unique number associated with each *interrupt.*

interrupt vector

The address of an *interrupt service routine.*

interrupt vector table

A table containing *interrupt vectors* and indexed by *interrupt type.* This table contains the *processor's* mapping between *interrupts* and *interrupt service routines* and must be initialized by the programmer.

intertask communication

A mechanism used by *tasks* and *interrupt service routines* to share information and synchronize their access to shared resources. The most common building blocks of intertask communication are *semaphores* and *mutexes.*

linker

A software development tool that accepts one or more *object files* as input and outputs a *relocatable* program. The linker is thus run after all of the source files have been compiled or assembled.

locator

A software development tool that assigns *physical addresses* to the *relocatable* program produced by the *linker.* This is the last step in the preparation of software for execution by an *embedded system,* and the resulting file is called an *executable.* In some cases, the locator's function is hidden within the *linker.*

logic analyzer

A hardware debugging tool that can be used to capture the logic levels (0 or 1) of dozens, or even hundreds, of electrical signals in real time. Logic analyzers can be quite helpful for debugging hardware problems and complex *processor-peripheral* interactions.

memory map

A table or diagram containing the name and address range of each *peripheral* addressable by the *processor* within the *memory space*. Memory maps are a helpful aid in getting to know the hardware.

memory-mapped I/O

Common hardware design methodology in which *I/O devices* are placed into the *memory space* rather than the *I/O space*. From the *processor's* point of view, memory-mapped I/O devices look very much like memory devices.

memory space

A *processor's* standard address space. Contrast with *I/O space*.

microcontroller

A microcontroller is very similar to a *microprocessor*. The main difference is that a microcontroller is designed specifically for use in *embedded systems*. Microcontrollers typically include a *CPU*, memory (a small amount of *RAM*, *ROM*, or both), and other *peripherals* on the same chip. Common examples are the 8051, Intel's 80196, and Motorola's 68HCxx series.

microprocessor

A piece of silicon containing a general-purpose *CPU*. The most common examples are Intel's 80x86 and Motorola's 680x0 families.

monitor

In the context of this book, a *debug monitor*. However, there is a second meaning for this word that is associated with *intertask communication*. In that context, a monitor is a language-level synchronization feature.

multiprocessing

The use of more than one *processor* in a single computer system. So-called "multiprocessor systems" usually have a common *memory space* through which the processors can communicate and share data. In addition, some multiprocessor systems support *parallel processing*.

multitasking

The execution of multiple software routines in pseudoparallel. Each routine represents a separate "thread of execution" and is referred to as a task. The *operating system* is responsible for simulating parallelism by parceling out the *processor's* time.

mutex

A data structure for *mutual exclusion*, also known as a *binary semaphore*. A mutex is basically a *multitasking*-aware binary flag that can be used to protect *critical sections* from interruption.

mutual exclusion

A guarantee of exclusive access to a shared resource. In *embedded systems*, the shared resource is typically a block of memory, a global variable, or a set of *registers*. Mutual exclusion can be achieved with the use of a *semaphore* or *mutex*.

NVRAM

Nonvolatile Random-Access Memory. A type of *RAM* that retains its data even when the system is powered down. NVRAM frequently consists of an *SRAM* and a long-life battery.

OTP

See *one-time programmable*.

object code

A set of *processor*-readable *opcodes* and data. The output of *compilers, assemblers, linkers,* and *locators* are files containing object code.

object file

A file containing *object code*. The output of a *compiler* or *assembler*.

one-time programmable

Any programmable device, like a *PROM*, that can be programmed just once by the end user. However, this term is used almost exclusively to refer to *microcontrollers* that have on-chip PROM.

opcode

A sequence of bits that is recognized by the *processor* as one of the instructions in its instruction set.

operating system

A piece of software that makes *multitasking* possible. An operating system typically consists of a set of function calls, or *software interrupts*, and a periodic clock tick. The operating system is responsible for deciding which task should be using the *processor* at a given time and for controlling access to shared resources.

oscilloscope

A hardware debugging tool that allows you to view the voltage on one or more electrical lines. For example, you might use an oscilloscope to determine if a particular *interrupt* is currently asserted.

PROM

Programmable Read-Only Memory. A type of *ROM* that can be written (programmed) with a *device programmer*. These memory devices can be programmed only once, so they are sometimes referred to as write-once or *one-time programmable* devices.

parallel processing

The ability to apply two or more *processors* to a single computation.

peripheral

A piece of hardware other than the processor, usually memory or an *I/O device*. The peripheral can reside within the same chip as the processor, in which case it is called an internal peripheral.

physical address

The actual address that is placed on the *address bus* when accessing a memory location or *register*.

preemptive

A *scheduler* is said to be preemptive if it allows the running *task* to be suspended when a higher-*priority* task becomes ready. Non-preemptive schedulers are easier to implement but less appropriate for embedded systems.

priority

The relative importance of one *task* compared to another.

priority inversion

An unwanted software situation in which a high-priority *task* is delayed while waiting for access to a shared resource that is not even being used at the time. For all practical purposes, the *priority* of this task has been lowered during the delay period.

process

A word that is often confused with *task* or *thread*. The crucial distinction is that all of the tasks in a system share a common memory space. Processes, on the other hand, always have their own private memory space. Processes are common in multi-user systems but are rarely, if ever, found in *embedded systems*.

processor

A generic term that does not distinguish between *microprocessor, microcontroller,* and *digital signal processor.* I have purposefully used this term throughout the book because the actual processor type has very little impact on the type of embedded software development described here.

processor family

A set of related *processors*, usually successive generations from the same manufacturer. For example, Intel's 80x86 family began with the 8086 and now includes the 80186, 286, 386, 486, Pentium, and many others. The later models in a family are typically backwards-compatible with the ones that came before.

processor-independent

A piece of software that is independent of the *processor* on which it will be run. Most programs that can be written in a *high-level language* are processor-independent. Contrast with *processor-specific*.

processor-specific

> A piece of software that is highly dependent on the *processor* on which it will be run. Such code must usually be written in *assembly language*. Contrast with *processor-independent*.

profiler

> A software development tool that collects and reports execution statistics for your programs. These statistics include the number of calls to each subroutine and the total amount of time spent within each. This data can be used to learn which subroutines are the most critical and, therefore, demand the greatest code efficiency.

program counter

> See *instruction pointer*.

RAM

> Random-Access Memory. A broad classification of memory devices that includes all devices in which individual memory locations can be read or written as required.

RISC

> Reduced Instruction Set Computer. Describes the architecture of a *processor family*. RISC processors generally feature fixed-length instructions, a load-store memory architecture, and a large number of general-purpose *registers* or register windows. The MIPS processor family is an excellent example. Contrast with *CISC*.

ROM

> Read-Only Memory. A broad classification of memory devices that includes all devices in which the individual memory locations can be read but not written.

ROM emulator

> A debugging tool that takes the place of—or emulates—the *ROM* on your *target* board. A ROM emulator acts very much like a *debug monitor*, except that it includes its own serial or network connection to the *host*.

ROM monitor

> See *debug monitor*.

RTOS

> Real-Time Operating System. An *operating system* designed specifically for use in *real-time systems*.

race condition

> A situation in which the outcome of a program can be affected by the exact order in which the instructions are executed. Race conditions are only an issue where *interrupts* and/or *preemption* are possible and where *critical sections* exist.

real-time system

Any computer system, embedded or otherwise, that has *deadlines*. The following question can be used to identify real-time systems: is a late answer as bad as, or even worse than, a wrong answer? In other words, what happens if the computation doesn't finish in time? If nothing bad happens, it's not a real-time system. If someone dies or the mission fails, it's generally considered "hard" real-time, which is meant to imply that the system has "hard" deadlines. Everything in between is "soft" real-time.

recursive

Refers to software that calls itself. Recursion should generally be avoided in an *embedded system* because it frequently requires a large *stack*.

reentrant

Refers to software that can be executed multiple times simultaneously. A reentrant function can be safely called *recursively* or from multiple *tasks*. The key to making code reentrant is to ensure *mutual exclusion* whenever accessing global variables or shared *registers*.

register

A memory location that is part of a *processor* or a *peripheral*. In other words, it's not normal memory. Generally, each bit or set of bits within the register controls some behavior of the larger device.

relocatable

A file containing *object code* that is almost ready for execution on the *target*. The final step is to use a *locator* to fix the remaining relocatable addresses within the code. The result of that process is an *executable*.

reset address

The address from which the first instruction will be fetched after the *processor* is powered on or reset.

reset code

A small piece of code that is placed at the *reset address*. The reset code is usually written in *assembly language* and might simply be the equivalent of "jump to the *startup code*."

reset vector

See *reset address*.

SRAM

Static Random-Access Memory. A type of *RAM* that retains its contents as long as power is supplied to it. Data stored in an SRAM is lost when the system is powered down or reset.

scheduler

    The part of an *operating system* that decides which *task* to run next. This decision is based on the readiness of each task, their relative *priorities*, and the specific scheduling algorithm implemented.

semaphore

    A data structure that is used for *intertask communication*. Semaphores are usually provided by the *operating system*.

simulator

    A debugging tool that runs on the *host* and pretends to be the *target processor*. A simulator can be used to test pieces of the software before the embedded hardware is available. Unfortunately, attempts to simulate interactions with complex *peripherals* are often more trouble than they are worth.

software interrupt

    An *interrupt* that is generated by a software instruction. Software interrupts are commonly used to implement *breakpoints* and *operating system* entry points. Compare with *trap*.

stack

    An area of memory that contains a last-in-first-out queue of storage for parameters, automatic variables, return addresses, and other information that must be maintained across function calls. In *multitasking* situations, each *task* generally has its own stack.

stack frame

    An area of the *stack* associated with a particular function call.

startup code

    A piece of *assembly language* code that prepares the way for software written in a *high-level language*. Most C/C++ *cross-compilers* come with startup code that you can modify, compile, and link with your embedded programs.

target

    Another name for the *embedded system*. This term is usually used during software development, to distinguish the embedded system from the *host* with which it communicates.

task

    The central abstraction of an *operating system*. Each task must maintain its own copy of the *instruction pointer* and general-purpose *registers*. Unlike *processes*, tasks share a common memory space and must be careful to avoid overwriting each other's code and data.

thread

    Another name for a *task*. This name is more common in *operating systems* that support *processes*. A task is simply a thread in a single-process system.

tracepoint

Similar to a *breakpoint* except that a counter is incremented rather than stopping the program. Tracepoints are not supported by all debugging tools.

trap

An interrupt that is generated by the *processor's* own internal hardware. For example, the processor might trap if an illegal *opcode* is found in your program. Compare with *software interrupt*.

volatile

A value that can change without the intervention of software is said to be volatile. For example, values within the *registers* of some *I/O devices* change in response to external events. C's `volatile` keyword should be used to warn your *compiler* about any pointers that point to such registers. This will ensure that the actual value is reread each time the data is used.

watchdog timer

A hardware timer that is periodically reset by software. If the software crashes or hangs, the watchdog timer will expire, and the entire system will be reset automatically.

Bibliography

One of the most frustrating aspects of developing embedded software is that there are few references available. Many of the books that have been written are poor or out of print, and there are only a handful of periodicals dedicated to the subject. What follows is an annotated list of the books, magazines, and other resources I found most helpful in writing this book. This is not an attempt to itemize all of the relevant publications. In fact, I have specifically omitted several books and magazines that did not impress me. What's left is a list of books worth owning, magazines and conferences worthy of your time, and World Wide Web sites worth bookmarking.

Books

Ball, Stuart R. *Embedded Microprocessor Systems: Real World Design*. Newton, Mass.: Butterworth-Heinemann, 1996.

> This tiny book is packed full of information about hardware design and embedded system development that every embedded software engineer should understand to be effective.

Brown, John Forrest. *Embedded Systems Programming in C and Assembly*. New York: Van Nostrand Reinhold, 1994.

> It's a good thing I didn't know about this book a few years ago. If I had, I might not have tried writing my own. It is obvious to me that Mr. Brown and I had similar visions for our books. And since I have tried to stay away from assembly language as much as possible, this book would make an excellent companion to the one you are reading.

Ganssle, Jack G. *The Art of Programming Embedded Systems*. San Diego: Academic Press, 1992.

Some very practical advice from one of our industry's most vocal gurus. The author of a monthly column in *Embedded Systems Programming* (described later in this bibliography), Mr. Ganssle has helpfully collected some of his most lasting tips and rules of thumb in this book. A handy reference for topics that are too specific to be covered here.

Kernighan, Brian W., and Dennis M. Ritchie. *The C Programming Language*. Englewood Cliffs, N.J.: Prentice-Hall, 1988.

A concise explanation of C's syntax and semantics direct from the founding fathers. A necessary component of any programmer's bookshelf.

Labrosse, Jean J. *µC/OS: The Real-Time Kernel*. Lawrence, Kans.: R & D Publications, 1992.

A real-time operating system with source code and explanatory text—all for the price of a book. A great investment for someone who's thinking of writing their own operating system, or just looking for free source code. µC/OS (pronounced "micro-COS") has been ported to many processors and has a large user base.

Rosenberg, Jonathan B. *How Debuggers Work: Algorithms, Data Structures, and Architecture*. New York: John P. Wiley & Sons, 1996.

If you've ever wondered what a debugger looks like on the inside, this book is for you. It will also give you a better understanding of the split between debugger and debug monitor and the potential for interference between the debugger and your programs.

Satir, Gregory, and Doug Brown. *C++: The Core Language*. Cambridge, Mass.: O'Reilly & Associates, 1995.

An excellent introduction to C++ for competent C programmers. If you don't already have a C++ book that you like, try this one.

Van der Linden, Peter. *Expert C Programming: Deep C Secrets*. Englewood Cliffs, N.J.: Prentice-Hall, 1994.

Written by a member of Sun Microsystems' compiler development team, this book helps to fill the gaps in knowledge between an ordinary C programmer and a guru. Although not entirely necessary, an understanding of these advanced topics can only make you a better embedded programmer. This book is an excellent reference as well as an entertaining read.

Van Sickle, Ted. *Programming Microcontrollers in C.* Solana Beach, Calif.: HighText Publications, 1994.

Like many of the embedded programming books that I've found, this one is specific to a particular processor family. However, because the book is well written and Motorola's microcontrollers are quite popular, some readers will still find it useful.

Magazines and Conferences

Embedded Systems Programming

A monthly publication devoted specifically to the issues embedded software developers face on the job. Every article and column is packed with practical advice and written in a casual style familiar to readers of this and other Nutshell Handbooks. I highly recommend that everyone reading this sentence immediately put my book down and take a few minutes to sign up for a free subscription at *http://www.embedded.com/mag.shtml*. It usually takes several months to get going, but is well worth the wait.

In addition, you might want to purchase a copy of the CD-ROM archive. This searchable database contains hundreds of past articles and columns and was an indispensable reference in the creation of this book. More information is available at *http://www.embedded.com/cd.htm*.

Embedded Systems Conference

A technical conference hosted several times each year by the publishers of the magazine just described. The conference has been running for about 10 years, and the number of exhibitors and attendees continues to grow each year. The knowledge to be gained here far outweighs the cost of traveling to the conference and attending the classes. I try to go as often as I can.

World Wide Web

Chip Directory (http://www.hitex.com/chipdir/)

An unbelievably large collection of information about common processors and peripherals. This is not the only such site on the Web, but it is one of the best maintained and it has links to many of the others.

CPU Info Center (http://infopad.eecs.berkeley.edu/CIC/)

Tons of information about new and old processors alike. Includes a section specifically about common embedded processors.

CRC Pitstop (http://www.ross.net/crc/)

A site dedicated to information about CRC implementation, including Ross Williams' "Painless Guide to CRC Error Detection Algorithms." The latter is the most readable explanation of CRC calculations I've ever found.

Electronic Engineers' Toolbox (http://www.eetoolbox.com/ebox.htm)

Focused on embedded systems, real-time software development issues, and Internet-enabling technologies, the "EE Toolbox" is designed to make your job easier. The publishers of this site have identified, indexed, and summarized thousands of relevant Internet resources and brought them all together in one place.

Embedded Intel Architecture (http://www.intel.com/design/intarch/)

Intel's home page for their embedded processor line, including the 80188EB. In addition to technical information about the hardware, there are also free development and debugging tools and example source code listings.

news:comp.arch.embedded

A newsgroup devoted to many of the topics discussed in this book. Discussions frequently involve software development tools and processes, comparisons of commercial real-time operating systems, and suggestions for processor selection criteria.

news:comp.realtime

Another good newsgroup for embedded systems discussion. This one tends to focus more heavily on real-time scheduling issues, however, so not all of the information is relevant. A list of FAQs from this group can be found at *http://www.faqs.org/faqs/by-newsgroup/comp/comp.realtime.html*.

Index

Numbers

80188EB processor (Intel), 51–53, 55
80x86 family (Intel), 51

A

Ada, 10
address bus, 151
address bus tests, 68–70
addresses vs. pointers, 46
ADEOS (example), 101–119
    clock tick, 109
    context switch (see context switches)
    mutexes, 116–119, 157
    ready list, 110
    scheduler (see scheduler)
    scheduling, 108–113
    scheduling points, 109
    tasks (see tasks)
AMD 29F010 Flash memory, 80
APIs (application programming
        interfaces), 107
application software, 151
Arcom board, 11, 149–150
    AMD 29F010 Flash memory, 80
    debug monitor, 34–35
    Intel 80188EB processor, 51–53, 55
    interupt map, 49
    I/O map, 45
    LEDs, 15

    memory map, 44
    Zilog 85230 serial controller, 137–138
as (GNU assembler), 22
ASIC, 151
assembler, 151
assembly, 10, 151
    hand-coded, optimizing, 141
    inline assembly, 16
    startup code, 24

B

bcc (Borland's C++ Compiler), 27
binary semaphore, 151
Blinking LED program (example), 14–18,
        126–130
    building, 27–29
    debugging, 34
    Timer class with, 97–99
board support package, 151
Borland's C++ Compiler, 27
Borland's Turbo Assembler, 27
Borland's Turbo Debugger, 34–35
breakpoints, 36, 152
build process, 19–27
    Blinking LED program (example), 27–29
    compiling, 21–23
    converting programs to binary, 25–27
    linking object files, 23–25
byte-oriented communication, 33

C

C, 9–11
    pointers vs. addresses, 46
    startup code, 24
C++, 9–11
    classes, 146
    constructors, 147
    default parameter values, 146
    destructors, 147
    operator overloading, 147
    performance penalty, 146–148
    pointers vs. addresses, 46
    polymorphism, 148
    startup code, 24
    virtual functions, 148
C-front technology, 146
checksums, 74
CircBuf class, 138
CISC, 152
clock ticks, 109
code optimization, 139–148
    dead code elimination, 143
    decreasing code size, 139–140, 143–144
    increasing efficiency, 142
    reducing memory usage, 144
COFF (Common Object File Format), 22
commercial operating systems, 122–123
compiler, 152
compiling programs, 21–23
    Blinking LED program (example), 28
    optimization, 139–142
context, task, 102, 152
context switches, 113–114, 122, 152
control registers, 84–86
converting programs to binary, 25–27
cost of development, 5
cost of production, 5
counting semaphore, 152
CPU, 152
CRCs (cyclic redundancy codes), 75–79
    as checksums, 74
critical sections, 105, 119, 152
cross-compilers, 22, 152
    startup code, 24
crt0.s file, 24
cyclic redundancy codes (CRCs), 75–79

D

Das Blinkenlights (see Blinking LED
    program)
data bus, 153
data bus tests, 66–68
data structures overlaying registers, 87
dead code elimination, 143
deadline, 153
deadlock, 120, 153
debug monitor, 153
debugger, 153
debugging
    debug monitors, 32–33
        emulators vs., 36
    hardware testing, tools for, 38–39
    LED as success indicator, 31
    logic analyzers and oscilloscopes, 38–39
    optimized programs and, 143
    remote debuggers, 32–35
    simulators, 37
decrement test, 71–72
default parameter values, 146
delay( ) (example), 17–18
dereferencing memory, 145
design requirements, 5–6
development cost, 5
device drivers, 86–89, 153
    Timer driver (example), 89–99
    tracking state of, 88
device programmer, 30, 59–60, 154
device registers, 84–86
digital signal processors (DSPs), 51, 153
digital watches, 7
direct memory access (DMA), 62
disabling interrupts, 122
DMA (direct memory access), 62, 152
downloading embedded software
    remote debuggers for, 32–35
    into ROM, 30–32
DRAM, 58, 153
DRAM controllers, 59
DSPs (digital signal processors), 51, 153

E

EEPROM, 60, 154
electrical wiring problems, 63–64

ELF (Extended Linker Format), 22
embedded C++ standard, 10, 147
embedded operating systems, 100–123
   ADEOS (example), 101–119
   real-time, 119–122
   selecting third-party, 122–123
embedded systems, defined, 1–8, 154
emulators, 35–36, 74, 154
EPROM, 60, 154
executable, 154
external peripherals, 53–54

F

FIFO scheduling, 106
filesystem, creating with Flash memory, 83
firmware, 154
fixed-point arithmetic, 142
Flash drivers, 80–83
Flash memory, 31, 60, 79–83, 154
   creating filesystem with, 83
floating-point calculations, 142

G

gcc (GNU C/C++ compiler), 22
gdb (GBU debugger), 33
general-purpose computers, 1–2, 155
global variables, 142
GNU tools
   assembler (as), 22
   compiler (gcc), 22
   debugger (gdb), 33
   linker (ld), 23
goto statements, 144

H

hand-coded assembly, 141
hardware, 11–12, 40–56
   breakpoints, 36
   debugging, 38–39
   device drivers and, 86
   electrical wiring problems, 63–64
   external peripherals, 53–54
   initializing, 54–56, 88, 91
   input and output devices, 14
   processors, 42–53
   tracking state of, 88
   troubleshooting, 54

header files for boards, 45, 47
headers of object files, 23
heap, 155
heap size, limiting, 145
"Hello, World!" program (example), 13–14, 124–138
.hex files, 29
high-level language, 155
HLL, 155
host, 155
hybrid memory devices, 60–61, 145

I

i8018xEB class, 92
ICE, 155
idle task, 110
improperly inserted memory chips, 65
in-circuit emulators (ICEs), 35–36
increment test, 71–72
infinite loops, role of, 18
initializing
   DRAM, 59
   hardware, 54–56, 88, 91
inline assembly, 16
inline functions, 140
input and output, 4
   I/O map, 45–47
   output devices, 14
instruction pointer, 156
Intel 80188EB processor, 51–53, 55
Intel 80x86 family, 51
Intel Hex Format, 29
interrupt keyword, 94
interrupt latency, 156
interrupt service routines (ISRs), 48–50, 88, 121, 142, 145, 156
interrupt type, 156
interrupt vector, 156
interrupt vector table, 156
interrupts, 48–50, 156
   interrupt maps, 49
   latency, 121
intertask communication, 156
I/O, 155
I/O device, 155
I/O map, 155
I/O-mapped registers, 85–86
I/O space, 155

"irrelevant code" elimination, 143
ISRs (interrupt service routines), 48–50, 88,
      121, 142, 145, 155

J

Java, 107

L

latency, interrupt, 121
ld (GNU linker), 23
LED as success indicator, 31
libgloss package (GNU), 24
library routines, 144
lifetime of system, 6
linkers, 23–25, 156
linking object files, 23–25
    Blinking LED program (example), 28
locators, 25–27, 156
logic analyzers, 38–39, 156
loops, infinite, 18

M

map files, 28
Mars Pathfinder, 8
memory, 5, 57–83
    DMA (direct memory access), 62
    Flash memory, 31, 60, 79–83
    improperly inserted chips, 65
    missing chips, 64
    peripherals vs., 43
    pointers vs. addresses, 46
    reducing usage of, 144
    testing, 61–74
        address bus, 68–70
        common problems, 63–65
        data bus, 66–68
        device, 71
        example of, 72–74
        test strategy, 65–74
    types of, 57–61
    validating contents of, 74–79
memory map, 43–45, 157
memory-mapped I/O, 157
memory-mapped registers, 85–86
memory space, 157
microcontrollers, 51, 157
microprocessors, 2, 51, 157
missing memory chips, 64

monitor, 157
multiprocessing, 157
multitasking, 102–106, 157
    context switches, 113–114, 122
    deadlock and priority inversion, 120
    scheduler, 104, 106–113
    synchronization, 114–119
Mutex class (example), 116
mutexes, 114–119, 157
mutual exclusion, 157

N

native compilers, 22, 24
native word size, 144
newlib package (Cygnus), 25
NVRAM, 61, 158

O

object code, 158
object files, 22, 158
    contents of, 22
    headers, 23
    linking, 23–25
        Blinking LED program (example), 28
    reset code, 54
    startup code, 23–24, 28, 56
on-chip peripherals, 51–53
one-time programmable (OTP) devices, 60,
    158
opcode, 158
operating systems, 100–123, 158
    ADEOS (example), 101–119
    context switches, 113–114, 122
    deadlock, 120
    priority inversion, 120
    real-time, 3, 119–122, 145
    schedulers, 104, 106–113
    selecting third-party, 122–123
    synchronization, 114–119
optimizing code, 139–148
    dead code elimination, 143
    decreasing code size, 139–140, 143–144
    increasing efficiency, 142
    reducing memory usage, 144
oscilloscopes, 38–39, 158
OTP devices, 60, 158
output (see input and output)
overlapping memory locations, 68–70

P

P2LTCH register (Arcom board), 15–17
parallel processing, 158
Pathfinder mission (NASA), 8
PCB (peripheral control block), 51
performance
    C++ language penalty, 146–148
    optimizing code, 139–148
    real-time systems, 120
peripherals, 84–99, 159
    control and status registers, 84–86
    device driver design, 86–89
    external, 53–54
    on-chip, 51–53
    Timer driver (example), 89–99
    tracking state of, 88
physical address, 159
platforms, 11
pointers to device registers, 85
pointers vs. addresses, 46
polling, 48, 142
"power-of-two" addresses, 68
preemptive scheduling, 107–108, 159
printing text strings (example), 130–131
priority, 159
priority-based scheduling, 108
priority inversion, 120, 159
process, 159
processor family, 159
processor-independent, 159
processors, 50–53, 159
    communicating with, 47–50
    electrical wiring problems, 63–64
    emulating, 35–36, 74
    examining, 42–47
    Intel 80188EB, 51–53, 55
    processing power, 5
production cost, 5
profilers, 140, 160
program counter, 160
programs
    debugging
        emulators, 35–36, 74
        remote debuggers, 32–35
        simulators for, 37
    downloading into ROM, 30–32
    software build process (see build
        process)
PROM, 59, 158

R

race condition, 160
RAM, 58, 144, 160
ready list, 110
readyList class, 106, 110
real-time systems, 3, 119–122, 145, 160–161
real-time tracing, 36
recursive, 161
reentrant, 161
references, unresolved, 23–25
register, 161
register variables, 142
reliability of system, 6
relocatable, 161
remote debuggers, 32–35
reset address, 161
reset code, 54, 161
reset vector, 161
RISC, 160
ROM, 160
    downloading software into, 30–32
    inserting into the board, 31
    reducing usage, 144
    ROM emulators, 36, 160
    ROM monitor, 160
    types of, 59
round robin scheduling, 107
RTOS (see real-time systems)
running task, 103

S

SCC class, 138
SCC (serial communications
        controller), 131
    Zilog 85230, 137–138
Sched class (example), 108
scheduler, 104, 106–113, 162
scheduling points, 109
semaphores, 115, 162
serial ports, 130–137
    Zilog 85230 serial controller, 137–138
SerialPort class (example), 130, 132–137
shortest-job-first scheduling, 107
simulators, 37, 162
size of code, decreasing, 139–140, 143–144
software
    build process (see build process)
    infinite loops, role of, 18

software (*continued*)
  optimizing code, 139–148
  platforms, 11
  (see also operating systems)
software interrupt, 162
SRAM, 58, 161
  testing (example), 72–74
stack, 162
stack frame, 162
stack size reductions, 145
standard library routines, 144
startup code, 23–24, 28, 56, 162
  hardware initialization and, 54
startup.asm file, 24, 28
startup.obj file, 28
states of operating system tasks, 103
status registers, 84–86
strings, printing (example), 130–131
structures overlaying registers, 87
switch statement, 140
symbol tables, 23
symbols, unresolved, 23–25
synchronization, 114–119

T

table lookups, 140
target, 162
Target188EB board (see Arcom board)
Task class, 103
TaskList class, 106
tasks, 101–106, 162
  ADEOS (example), 103–104
  context switches, 113–114, 122
  deadlock, 120
  priority inversion, 120
  scheduler, 104, 106–113
  states of, 103
  synchronization, 114–119
  task control blocks, 103
tasm (Borland's Turbo Assembler), 28
tcrom locator, 29
tdr command, 35
testing memory, 61–74
  common problems, 63–65
  example of, 72–74
  test strategy, 65–74

text, printing (example), 130–131
thread, 162
Timer class (example), 89–91, 127
  Blinking LED with, 97–99
Timer driver (example), 89–99
TimerCounter data structure (example), 87
tlink command, 28
tload utility, 34
tracepoint, 163
tracing, real-time, 36
tracking hardware/driver state, 88
trap, 163
troubleshooting
  deadlock and priority inversion, 120
  hardware, 54
  memory testing, 61–74
    common problems, 63–65
    example of, 72–74
    test strategy, 65–74
  validating memory contents, 74–79
  watchdog timers, 98
Turbo Assembler (Borland), 27
Turbo Debugger (Borland), 34–35

U

unresolved symbols/references, 23–25

V

validating memory contents, 74–79
variables
  code efficiency and, 142
  registers to resemble, 85
video game players, 7
volatile keyword, 85, 163

W

waiting (doing nothing), 17–18, 103
walking 1's test, 66
watchdog timers, 98, 163
wiring problems, 63–64
word size, 144
worst-case performance, 120–121

Z

Zilog 85230 serial controller, 44, 137–138

About the Author

Michael Barr is the founder and president of Netrino, a provider of software engineering services and shareware for embedded systems. Netrino encourages all of its employees to share their technical expertise by writing magazine articles and books and by speaking at industry conferences. An archive of these various publications is maintained on their web site, at *http://www.netrino.com*.

Michael earned B.S. and M.S. degrees in electrical engineering from the University of Maryland. He has spent most of his career so far developing embedded software, device drivers, and real-time operating systems. Michael also enjoys writing and teaching and looks forward to starting his next book; he is currently considering several ideas, including at least one novel.

Colophon

The insects on the cover of *Programming Embedded Systems in C and C++* are ticks. There are approximately 850 species of these small to microscopic, blood-feeding parasites distributed worldwide. They are particularly abundant in tropical and subtropical regions. There are two main families of ticks: hard ticks, whose mouth parts are visible from above, and soft ticks, whose mouth parts are hidden.

In both hard and soft ticks, the mouth is made up of three major parts: the palps, the chelicerae, and the hypostome. It is the hypostome that is inserted into the host's skin while the tick is feeding. A series of backward-facing projections on the hypostome make it difficult to remove the tick from the skin. Most ticks also secrete a sticky substance that glues them into place. This substance dissolves when the tick is done feeding. Their external body surface expands from 200 to 600 percent to accommodate the blood that is ingested.

Ticks go through three life stages: larva, nymph, and adult. At each stage they feed on a mammal, reptile, or bird host. Ticks wait for a host by perching on leaves or other surfaces with their front two legs extended. When a host brushes up against them they latch on and attach themselves. Adult female hard ticks lay a single batch of thousands of eggs and then die. Adult male ticks also die after a single mating.

As parasites go, ticks can be very nasty. They transmit more disease than any other blood-sucking parasite, including Lyme disease, Rocky Mountain spotted fever, and relapsing fever. They can also cause excessive blood loss. Some ticks secrete nerve poisons that can potentially cause death. A tick can be removed from skin by grasping it with a tweezer or a special tick-removing device as close to the skin as possible, and pulling in one steady motion. Do not squeeze the tick. Immediately flush it down the toilet—or place it in a sealed container and hold onto it for one month, in case you develop symptoms of a disease.

Melanie Wang was the production editor and proofreader for *Embedded Programming Systems in C and C++*. Sheryl Avruch was the production manager; Paulette A. Miley was the copy editor; Nancy Kotary and Madeleine Newell provided quality control. Seth Maislin wrote the index.

Edie Freedman designed the cover of this book, using a 19th-century engraving from the Dover Pictorial Archive. The cover layout was produced with QuarkXPress 3.3 using the ITC Garamond font.

The inside layout was designed by Edie Freedman and implemented in FrameMaker by Mike Sierra. The text and heading fonts are ITC Garamond Light and Garamond Book. The illustrations that appear in the book were created in Macromedia Freehand 7.0 by Robert Romano. This colophon was written by Clairemarie Fisher O'Leary.

Whenever possible, our books use a durable and flexible lay-flat binding, either RepKover™ or Otabind™. If the page count exceeds the maximum bulk possible for this type of binding, perfect binding is used.

More Titles from O'Reilly

C and C++

C++: The Core Language

By Gregory Satir & Doug Brown
1st Edition October 1995
228 pages, ISBN 1-56592-116-X

A first book for C programmers transitioning to C++, an object-oriented enhancement of the C programming language. Designed to get readers up to speed quickly, this book thoroughly explains the important concepts and features and gives brief overviews of the rest of the language. Covers features common to all C++ compilers, including those on UNIX, Windows NT, Windows, DOS, and Macs.

Practical C++ Programming

By Steve Oualline
1st Edition September 1995
584 pages, ISBN 1-56592-139-9

A complete introduction to the C++ language for the beginning programmer and C programmers transitioning to C++. This book emphasizes a practical, real-world approach, including how to debug, how to make your code understandable to others, and how to understand other people's code. Covers good programming style, C++ syntax (what to use and what not to use), C++ class design, debugging and optimization, and common programming mistakes.

Checking C Programs with lint

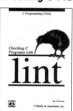

By Ian F. Darwin
1st Edition October 1988
84 pages, ISBN 0-937175-30-7

The *lint* program is one of the best tools for finding portability problems and certain types of coding errors in C programs. This handbook introduces you to *lint*, guides you through running it on your programs, and helps you interpret *lint's* output.

Practical C Programming, 3rd Edition

By Steve Oualline
3rd Edition August 1997
454 pages, ISBN 1-56592-306-5

Practical C Programming teaches you not only the mechanics of programming, but also how to create programs that are easy to read, maintain, and debug. This third edition introduces popular Integrated Development Environments on Windows systems, as well as UNIX programming utilities, and features a large statistics-generating program to pull together the concepts and features in the language.

High Performance Computing, 2nd Edition

By Kevin Dowd & Charles Severance
2nd Edition July 1998
466 pages, ISBN 1-56592-312-X

This new edition of *High Performance Computing* gives a thorough overview of the latest workstation and PC architectures and the trends that will influence the next generation. It pays special attention to memory design, tuning code for the best performance, multiprocessors, and benchmarking.

Java

Java in a Nutshell, Second Edition

By David Flanagan
2nd Edition May 1997
628 pages, ISBN 1-56592-262-X

This second edition of the bestselling Java book describes all the classes in the Java 1.1 API, with the exception of the still-evolving Enterprise APIs. And it still has all the great features that have made this the Java book most often recommended on the Internet: practical real-world examples and compact reference information. It's the only quick reference you'll need.

O'REILLY®

TO ORDER: **800-998-9938** • *order@oreilly.com* • *http://www.oreilly.com/*
OUR PRODUCTS ARE AVAILABLE AT A BOOKSTORE OR SOFTWARE STORE NEAR YOU.
FOR INFORMATION: **800-998-9938** • **707-829-0515** • *info@oreilly.com*

Java

Java in a Nutshell, DELUXE EDITION

By David Flanagan, et al.
1st Edition June 1997
628 pages, includes CD-ROM & book
ISBN 1-56592-304-9

Java in a Nutshell, Deluxe Edition, brings together on CD-ROM five volumes for Java developers and programmers, linking related info across books. *Exploring Java, 2nd Edition,* covers Java basics. *Java Language Reference, 2nd Edition, Java Fundamental Classes Reference,* and *Java AWT Reference* provide a definitive set of documentation on the Java language and the Java 1.1 core API. *Java in a Nutshell, 2nd Edition,* our bestselling quick reference, is included both on the CD-ROM and in a companion desktop edition. This deluxe library is an indispensable resource for anyone doing serious programming with Java 1.1.

Java Cryptography

By Jonathan B. Knudsen
1st Edition May 1998
362 pages, ISBN 1-56592-402-9

Java Cryptography teaches you how to write secure programs using Java's cryptographic tools. It includes thorough discussions of the java.security package and the Java Cryptography Extensions (JCE), showing you how to use security providers and even implement your own provider. It discusses authentication, key management, public and private key encryption, and includes a secure talk application that encrypts all data sent over the network. If you work with sensitive data, you'll find this book indispensable.

Java Security

By Scott Oaks
1st Edition May 1998
474 pages, ISBN 1-56592-403-7

This essential Java 1.2 book covers Java's security mechanisms and teaches you how to work with them. It discusses class loaders, security managers, access lists, digital signatures, and authentication and shows how to use these to create and enforce your own security policy.

Java Network Programming

By Elliotte Rusty Harold
1st Edition February 1997
442 pages, ISBN 1-56592-227-1

The network is the soul of Java. Most of what is new and exciting about Java centers around the potential for new kinds of dynamic, networked applications. *Java Network Programming* teaches you to work with Sockets, write network clients and servers, and gives you an advanced look at the new areas like multicasting, using the server API, and RMI. Covers Java 1.1.

Java Virtual Machine

By Jon Meyer & Troy Downing
1st Edition March 1997
452 pages, includes diskette
ISBN 1-56592-194-1

This book is a comprehensive programming guide for the Java Virtual Machine (JVM). It gives readers a strong overview and reference of the JVM so that they may create their own implementations of the JVM or write their own compilers that create Java object code. A Java assembler is provided with the book, so the examples can all be compiled and executed.

Java Swing

By Robert Eckstein, Marc Loy & Dave Wood
1st Edition September 1998
1252 pages, ISBN 1-56592-455-X

The Swing classes eliminate Java's biggest weakness: its relatively primitive user interface toolkit. Java Swing helps you to take full advantage of the Swing classes, providing detailed descriptions of every class and interface in the key Swing packages. It shows you how to use all of the new components, allowing you to build state-of-the-art user interfaces and giving you the context you need to understand what you're doing. It's more than documentation; Java Swing helps you develop code quickly and effectively.

O'REILLY®

TO ORDER: **800-998-9938** • *order@oreilly.com* • *http://www.oreilly.com/*

OUR PRODUCTS ARE AVAILABLE AT A BOOKSTORE OR SOFTWARE STORE NEAR YOU.

FOR INFORMATION: **800-998-9938** • **707-829-0515** • *info@oreilly.com*

Java

Java Threads

By Scott Oaks and Henry Wong
1st Edition January 1997
268 pages, ISBN 1-56592-216-6

With this book, you'll learn how to take full advantage of Java's thread facilities: where to use threads to increase efficiency, how to use them effectively, and how to avoid common mistakes like deadlock and race conditions. Covers Java 1.1.

Java Language Reference, Second Edition

By Mark Grand
2nd Edition July 1997
492 pages, ISBN 1-56592-326-X

This book helps you understand the subtle nuances of Java—from the definition of data types to the syntax of expressions and control structures—so you can ensure your programs run exactly as expected. The second edition covers the new language features that have been added in Java 1.1, such as inner classes, class literals, and instance initializers.

Java Fundamental Classes Reference

By Mark Grand & Jonathan Knudsen
1st Edition May 1997
1114 pages, ISBN 1-56592-241-7

The *Java Fundamental Classes Reference* provides complete reference documentation on the core Java 1.1 classes that comprise the *java.lang, java.io, java.net, java.util, java.text, java.math, java.lang.reflect,* and *java.util.zip* packages. Part of O'Reilly's Java documentation series, this edition describes Version 1.1 of the Java Development Kit. It includes easy-to-use reference material and provides lots of sample code to help you learn by example.

Java Servlet Programming

By Jason Hunter with
William Crawford
1st Edition November 1998
528 pages, ISBN 1-56592-391-X

Java servlets offer a fast, powerful, portable replacement for CGI scripts. *Java Servlet Programming* covers everything you need to know to write effective servlets. Topics include: serving dynamic Web content, maintaining state information, session tracking, database connectivity using JDBC, and applet-servlet communication.

Java Distributed Computing

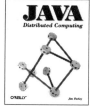

By Jim Farley
1st Edition January 1998
384 pages, ISBN 1-56592-206-9

Java Distributed Computing offers a general introduction to distributed computing, meaning programs that run on two or more systems. It focuses primarily on how to structure and write distributed applications and, therefore, discusses issues like designing protocols, security, working with databases, and dealing with low bandwidth situations.

Java Examples in a Nutshell

By David Flanagan
1st Edition September 1997
414 pages, ISBN 1-56592-371-5

From the author of *Java in a Nutshell*, this companion book is chock full of practical real-world programming examples to help novice Java programmers and experts alike explore what's possible with Java 1.1. If you learn best by example, this is the book for you.

How to stay in touch with O'Reilly

1. Visit Our Award-Winning Web Site

http://www.oreilly.com/

★ "Top 100 Sites on the Web" —*PC Magazine*
★ "Top 5% Web sites" —*Point Communications*
★ "3-Star site" —*The McKinley Group*

Our web site contains a library of comprehensive product information (including book excerpts and tables of contents), downloadable software, background articles, interviews with technology leaders, links to relevant sites, book cover art, and more. File us in your Bookmarks or Hotlist!

2. Join Our Email Mailing Lists

New Product Releases

To receive automatic email with brief descriptions of all new O'Reilly products as they are released, send email to: **listproc@online.oreilly.com**
Put the following information in the first line of your message (*not* in the Subject field):
subscribe oreilly-news

O'Reilly Events

If you'd also like us to send information about trade show events, special promotions, and other O'Reilly events, send email to:
listproc@online.oreilly.com
Put the following information in the first line of your message (*not* in the Subject field):
subscribe oreilly-events

3. Get Examples from Our Books via FTP

There are two ways to access an archive of example files from our books:

Regular FTP

*   ftp to:
    ftp.oreilly.com
    (login: anonymous
    password: your email address)
*   Point your web browser to:
    ftp://ftp.oreilly.com/

FTPMAIL

*   Send an email message to:
    ftpmail@online.oreilly.com
    (Write "help" in the message body)

4. Contact Us via Email

order@oreilly.com
To place a book or software order online. Good for North American and international customers.

subscriptions@oreilly.com
To place an order for any of our newsletters or periodicals.

books@oreilly.com
General questions about any of our books.

software@oreilly.com
For general questions and product information about our software. Check out O'Reilly Software Online at **http://software.oreilly.com/** for software and technical support information. Registered O'Reilly software users send your questions to: **website-support@oreilly.com**

cs@oreilly.com
For answers to problems regarding your order or our products.

booktech@oreilly.com
For book content technical questions or corrections.

proposals@oreilly.com
To submit new book or software proposals to our editors and product managers.

international@oreilly.com
For information about our international distributors or translation queries. For a list of our distributors outside of North America check out:
http://www.oreilly.com/www/order/country.html

O'Reilly & Associates, Inc.
101 Morris Street, Sebastopol, CA 95472 USA
TEL   707-829-0515 or 800-998-9938
           (6am to 5pm PST)
FAX   707-829-0104

O'REILLY®

Titles from O'Reilly

WEB

Advanced Perl Programming
Apache: The Definitive Guide,
    2nd Edition
ASP in a Nutshell
Building Your Own Web Conferences
Building Your Own Website™
CGI Programming with Perl
Designing with JavaScript
Dynamic HTML:
    The Definitive Reference
Frontier: The Definitive Guide
HTML: The Definitive Guide,
    3rd Edition
Information Architecture
    for the World Wide Web
JavaScript Pocket Reference
JavaScript: The Definitive Guide,
    3rd Edition
Learning VB Script
Photoshop for the Web
WebMaster in a Nutshell
WebMaster in a Nutshell,
    Deluxe Edition
Web Design in a Nutshell
Web Navigation:
    Designing the User Experience
Web Performance Tuning
Web Security & Commerce
Writing Apache Modules

PERL

Learning Perl, 2nd Edition
Learning Perl for Win32 Systems
Learning Perl/TK
Mastering Algorithms with Perl
Mastering Regular Expressions
Perl5 Pocket Reference, 2nd Edition
Perl Cookbook
Perl in a Nutshell
Perl Resource Kit—UNIX Edition
Perl Resource Kit—Win32 Edition
Perl/TK Pocket Reference
Programming Perl, 2nd Edition
Web Client Programming with Perl

GRAPHICS & MULTIMEDIA

Director in a Nutshell
Encyclopedia of Graphics
    File Formats, 2nd Edition
Lingo in a Nutshell
Photoshop in a Nutshell
QuarkXPress in a Nutshell

USING THE INTERNET

AOL in a Nutshell
Internet in a Nutshell
Smileys
The Whole Internet for Windows95
The Whole Internet:
    The Next Generation
The Whole Internet
    User's Guide & Catalog

JAVA SERIES

Database Programming with
    JDBC and Java
Developing Java Beans
Exploring Java, 2nd Edition
Java AWT Reference
Java Cryptography
Java Distributed Computing
Java Examples in a Nutshell
Java Foundation Classes in a Nutshell
Java Fundamental Classes Reference
Java in a Nutshell, 2nd Edition
Java in a Nutshell, Deluxe Edition
Java I/O
Java Language Reference, 2nd Edition
Java Media Players
Java Native Methods
Java Network Programming
Java Security
Java Servlet Programming
Java Swing
Java Threads
Java Virtual Machine

UNIX

Exploring Expect
GNU Emacs Pocket Reference
Learning GNU Emacs, 2nd Edition
Learning the bash Shell, 2nd Edition
Learning the Korn Shell
Learning the UNIX Operating System,
    4th Edition
Learning the vi Editor, 6th Edition
Linux in a Nutshell
Linux Multimedia Guide
Running Linux, 2nd Edition
SCO UNIX in a Nutshell
sed & awk, 2nd Edition
Tcl/Tk in a Nutshell
Tcl/Tk Pocket Reference
Tcl/Tk Tools
The UNIX CD Bookshelf
UNIX in a Nutshell, System V Edition
UNIX Power Tools, 2nd Edition
Using csh & tcsh
Using Samba
vi Editor Pocket Reference
What You Need To Know:
    When You Can't Find Your
    UNIX System Administrator
Writing GNU Emacs Extensions

SONGLINE GUIDES

NetLaw   NetResearch
NetLearning   NetSuccess
NetLessons   NetTravel

SOFTWARE

Building Your Own WebSite™
Building Your Own Web Conference
WebBoard™ 3.0
WebSite Professional™ 2.0
PolyForm™

SYSTEM ADMINISTRATION

Building Internet Firewalls
Computer Security Basics
Cracking DES
DNS and BIND, 3rd Edition
DNS on WindowsNT
Essential System Administration
Essential WindowsNT
    System Administration
Getting Connected:
    The Internet at 56K and Up
Linux Network Administrator's Guide
Managing IP Networks with
    Cisco Routers
Managing Mailing Lists
Managing NFS and NIS
Managing the WindowsNT Registry
Managing Usenet
MCSE: The Core Exams in a Nutshell
MCSE: The Electives in a Nutshell
Networking Personal Computers
    with TCP/IP
Oracle Performance Tuning,
    2nd Edition
Practical UNIX & Internet Security,
    2nd Edition
PGP: Pretty Good Privacy
Protecting Networks with SATAN
sendmail, 2nd Edition
sendmail Desktop Reference
System Performance Tuning
TCP/IP Network Administration,
    2nd Edition
termcap & terminfo
The Networking CD Bookshelf
Using & Managing PPP
Virtual Private Networks
WindowsNT Backup & Restore
WindowsNT Desktop Reference
WindowsNT Event Logging
WindowsNT in a Nutshell
WindowsNT Server 4.0 for
    Netware Administrators
WindowsNT SNMP
WindowsNT TCP/IP Administration
WindowsNT User Administration
Zero Administration for Windows

X WINDOW

Vol. 1: Xlib Programming Manual
Vol. 2: Xlib Reference Manual
Vol. 3M: X Window System
    User's Guide, Motif Edition
Vol. 4M: X Toolkit Intrinsics
    Programming Manual,
    Motif Edition
Vol. 5: X Toolkit Intrinsics
    Reference Manual
Vol. 6A: Motif Programming Manual
Vol. 6B: Motif Reference Manual
Vol. 8 : X Window System
    Administrator's Guide

PROGRAMMING

Access Database Design and
    Programming
Advanced Oracle PL/SQL
    Programming with Packages
Applying RCS and SCCS
BE Developer's Guide
BE Advanced Topics
C++: The Core Language
Checking C Programs with lint
Developing Windows Error Messages
Developing Visual Basic Add-ins
Guide to Writing DCE Applications
High Performance Computing,
    2nd Edition
Inside the Windows 95 File System
Inside the Windows 95 Registry
lex & yacc, 2nd Edition
Linux Device Drivers
Managing Projects with make
Oracle8 Design Tips
Oracle Built-in Packages
Oracle Design
Oracle PL/SQL Programming,
    2nd Edition
Oracle Scripts
Oracle Security
Palm Programming:
    The Developer's Guide
Porting UNIX Software
POSIX Programmer's Guide
POSIX.4: Programming
    for the Real World
Power Programming with RPC
Practical C Programming, 3rd Edition
Practical C++ Programming
Programming Python
Programming with curses
Programming with GNU Software
Pthreads Programming
Python Pocket Reference
Software Portability with imake,
    2nd Edition
UML in a Nutshell
Understanding DCE
UNIX Systems Programming for SVR4
VB/VBA in a Nutshell: The Languages
Win32 Multithreaded Programming
Windows NT File System Internals
Year 2000 in a Nutshell

USING WINDOWS

Excel97 Annoyances
Office97 Annoyances
Outlook Annoyances
Windows Annoyances
Windows98 Annoyances
Windows95 in a Nutshell
Windows98 in a Nutshell
Word97 Annoyances

OTHER TITLES

PalmPilot: The Ultimate Guide

O'REILLY®

TO ORDER: **800-998-9938** • *order@oreilly.com* • *http://www.oreilly.com/*
OUR PRODUCTS ARE AVAILABLE AT A BOOKSTORE OR SOFTWARE STORE NEAR YOU.
FOR INFORMATION: **800-998-9938** • **707-829-0515** • *info@oreilly.com*

International Distributors

UK, EUROPE, MIDDLE EAST AND NORTHERN AFRICA (EXCEPT FRANCE, GERMANY, SWITZERLAND, & AUSTRIA)

INQUIRIES
International Thomson Publishing Europe
Berkshire House
168-173 High Holborn
London WC1V 7AA
United Kingdom
Tel: 44-1-71-497-1422
Fax: 44-1-71-497-1426

ORDERS
International Thomson Publishing Services, Ltd.
Cheriton House, North Way
Andover, Hampshire SP10 5BE
United Kingdom
Tel: 44-1-264-342-832 (UK)
Tel: 44-1-264-342-806 (outside UK)
Fax: 44-1-264-364-418 (UK)
Fax: 44-1-264-342-761 (outside UK)
Email: itpint@itps.co.uk

FRANCE

GEODIF
61, Bd Saint-Germain
75240 Paris Cedex 05, France
Tel: 33-1-44-41-46-16 (French books)
Tel: 33-1-44-41-11-87 (English books)
Fax: 33-1-44-41-11-44
Email: distribution@eyrolles.com

ORDERS
SODIS
128, av.du Mal de Lattre de Tassigny
77403 Lagny Cédex, France
Tel: 33-1-60-07-82-00
Fax: 33-1-64-30-32-27

INQUIRIES
Éditions O'Reilly
18 rue Séguier
75006 Paris, France
Tel: 33-1-40-51-52-30
Fax: 33-1-40-51-52-31
Email: france@editions-oreilly.fr

GERMANY, SWITZERLAND, AUSTRIA

INQUIRIES
O'Reilly Verlag
Balthasarstr. 81
D-50670 Köln, Germany
Tel: 49-221-973160-0
Fax: 49-221-973160-8
Email: anfragen@oreilly.de

ORDERS
International Thomson Publishing
Königswinterer Straße 418
53227 Bonn, Germany
Tel: 49-228-970240
Fax: 49-228-441342
Email: order@oreilly.de

CANADA (FRENCH LANGUAGE BOOKS)

Les Éditions Flammarion ltée
375, Avenue Laurier Ouest
Montréal (Québec) H2V 2K3
Tel: 00-1-514-277-8807
Fax: 00-1-514-278-2085
Email: info@flammarion.qc.ca

HONG KONG

City Discount Subscription Service, Ltd.
Unit D, 3rd Floor, Yan's Tower
27 Wong Chuk Hang Road
Aberdeen, Hong Kong
Tel: 852-2580-3539
Fax: 852-2580-6463
Email: citydis@ppn.com.hk

KOREA

Hanbit Media, Inc.
Sonyoung Bldg. 202
Yeksam-dong 736-36
Kangnam-ku
Seoul, Korea
Tel: 822-554-9610
Fax: 822-556-0363
Email: hant93@chollian.dacom.co.kr

SINGAPORE, MALAYSIA, THAILAND

Addison-Wesley Longman Singapore Pte., Ltd.
25 First Lok Yang Road
Singapore 629734
Tel: 65-268-2666
Fax: 65-268-7023
Email: Daniel.Loh@awl.com.sg

PHILIPPINES

Mutual Books, Inc.
429-D Shaw Boulevard
Mandaluyong City, Metro
Manila, Philippines
Tel: 632-725-7538
Fax: 632-721-3056
Email: mbikikog@mnl.sequel.net

TAIWAN

O'Reilly Taiwan
No. 3, Lane 131
Hang-Chow South Road
Section 1, Taipei, Taiwan
Tel: 886-2-23968990
Fax: 886-2-23968916
Email: benh@oreilly.com

CHINA

China National Publishing
Industry Trading Corporation
504 AnHuiLi, AnDingMenWai
P.O. Box 782
Beijing 100011, China P.R.
Tel: 86-10-6424-0483
Fax: 86-10-6421-4540
Email: frederic@oreilly.com

INDIA

Computer Bookshop (India) Pvt. Ltd.
190 Dr. D.N. Road, Fort
Bombay 400 001 India
Tel: 91-22-207-0989
Fax: 91-22-262-3551
Email: cbsbom@giasbm01.vsnl.net.in

JAPAN

O'Reilly Japan, Inc.
Kiyoshige Building 2F
12-Bancho, Sanei-cho
Shinjuku-ku
Tokyo 160-0008 Japan
Tel: 81-3-3356-5227
Fax: 81-3-3356-5261
Email: japan@oreilly.com

ALL OTHER ASIAN COUNTRIES

O'Reilly & Associates, Inc.
101 Morris Street
Sebastopol, CA 95472 USA
Tel: 707-829-0515
Fax: 707-829-0104
Email: order@oreilly.com

AUSTRALIA

WoodsLane Pty., Ltd.
7/5 Vuko Place
Warriewood NSW 2102
Australia
Tel: 61-2-9970-5111
Fax: 61-2-9970-5002
Email: info@woodslane.com.au

NEW ZEALAND

Woodslane New Zealand, Ltd.
21 Cooks Street (P.O. Box 575)
Waganui, New Zealand
Tel: 64-6-347-6543
Fax: 64-6-345-4840
Email: info@woodslane.com.au

SOUTH AFRICA

International Thomson South Africa
Building 18, Constantia Park
138 Sixteenth Road
(P.O. Box 2459)
Halfway House, 1685 South Africa
Tel: 27-11-805-4819
Fax: 27-11-805-3648

LATIN AMERICA

McGraw-Hill Interamericana
Editores, S.A. de C.V.
Cedro No. 512
Col. Atlampa
06450, Mexico, D.F.
Tel: 52-5-547-6777
Fax: 52-5-547-3336
Email: mcgraw-hill@infosel.net.mx

O'REILLY®

TO ORDER: **800-998-9938** • *order@oreilly.com* • *http://www.oreilly.com/*
OUR PRODUCTS ARE AVAILABLE AT A BOOKSTORE OR SOFTWARE STORE NEAR YOU.
FOR INFORMATION: **800-998-9938** • **707-829-0515** • *info@oreilly.com*

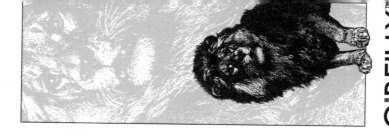

O'REILLY™

O'Reilly & Associates, Inc.
101 Morris Street
Sebastopol, CA 95472-9902
1-800-998-9938

Visit us online at:
http://www.ora.com/

O'REILLY WOULD LIKE TO HEAR FROM YOU

Which book did this card come from?

_____

Where did you buy this book?
- ❏ Bookstore
- ❏ Direct from O'Reilly
- ❏ Bundled with hardware/software
- ❏ Computer Store
- ❏ Class/seminar
- ❏ Other _____

What operating system do you use?
- ❏ UNIX
- ❏ Windows NT
- ❏ Other _____
- ❏ Macintosh
- ❏ PC(Windows/DOS)

What is your job description?
- ❏ System Administrator
- ❏ Network Administrator
- ❏ Web Developer
- ❏ Other _____
- ❏ Programmer
- ❏ Educator/Teacher

❏ Please send me O'Reilly's catalog, containing
a complete listing of O'Reilly books and
software.

Name _____ Company/Organization _____

Address _____

City _____ State _____ Zip/Postal Code _____ Country _____

Telephone _____ Internet or other email address (specify network) _____

eteenth century wood engraving
a bear from the O'Reilly &
ociates Nutshell Handbook®
ng & Managing UUCP.

POST CARD

NO POSTAGE
NECESSARY IF
MAILED IN THE
UNITED STATES

BUSINESS REPLY MAIL

FIRST CLASS MAIL   PERMIT NO. 80   SEBASTOPOL, CA

Postage will be paid by addressee

O'Reilly & Associates, Inc.
101 Morris Street
Sebastopol, CA 95472-9902